Bill Nye's Western Humor

Sketch of Bill Nye by Fred Opper

Bill Nye's Western Humor

Selected and with an introduction by
T. A. LARSON

Illustrated by
F. OPPER, J. H. SMITH, E. ZIMMERMAN

UNIVERSITY OF NEBRASKA PRESS · LINCOLN

Introduction Copyright © 1968 by the University of Nebraska Press
Library of Congress Catalog Card Number 67–20599

International Standard Book Number 0-8032-5821-6

First Printing June, 1968
First Bison Book Printing January, 1975
Most recent printing shown by first digit below:
1   2   3   4   5   6   7   8   9   10

Manufactured in the United States of America

Introduction

Edgar Wilson Nye, better known as Bill Nye, found himself and wrote his best humor during the seven years, 1876–1883, that he lived in Laramie, Wyoming Territory. Born in Maine in 1850, at the age of two he was taken to western Wisconsin where he grew up on a farm. After a secondary-school education he tried his hand with small success as a miller's helper, law clerk, teacher, and part-time reporter.

Not until he moved to Laramie when he was twenty-five did Nye find his true calling, writing humor. Later he recalled that "[in Wisconsin] where I lived I was still regarded as a boy." His son, Frank, in *Bill Nye: His Own Life Story*, judges that in Wisconsin parental repression and local conservatism stood in the way of his father's development as a humorist. These restraints fell away when Nye went West and became assistant editor of the *Laramie Daily Sentinel* in May, 1876.

Editor J. H. Hayford had been doing all the editorial work on the *Sentinel* by himself for seven years. When he hired Nye as his assistant at $12 a week, he did not know that he was getting a humorist. But he allowed Nye to write much as he pleased. The Nye columns that appeared in the *Sentinel* in 1876 and 1877 were not as well done, generally speaking, as those that appeared thereafter in other papers. Nye was practicing while on the *Sentinel*, and obviously was having a good time doing so.

Usually Hayford and Nye did not sign what they wrote; so it is not always possible to say who wrote what. When humor was attempted, however, Nye's inimitable style marked his columns. In his first week on the *Sentinel* the following appeared:

That choice season of the year has come when the venerable overshoe and the vacant castor-oil bottle are called upon to resign their respective positions in the backyard, and the house goes into a Committee of the Whole and investigates the cellar and the woodshed.

It is now time to dig pie plant and shake the luscious fruit from the asparagus tree.

The young man with the sorrel side whiskers and the mild skim-milk eye will proceed to coo the old, old story into the cleanest ear of his soul's idol.

The front gate will make ready for the spring campaign and prepare to support the united weight of two hearts that beat as one.

This little essay, which is unmistakably Nye's, has no local reference whatever, but before long local subjects began to receive attention. The frontier environment supplied attractive new themes for treatment by the transplanted Midwesterner. Novel situations and picturesque characters abounded in town and country. Laramie's 2,500 people included playful cronies and sympathetic critics. One in particular, Bill Root, spun yarns, a few of which, so it is said, Nye published with embellishments.

Six weeks after he arrived in Laramie, Nye learned something about frontier justice. A popular young sheepman was shot to death by "a sort of hermit" who worked for a cattle company. The murderer was soon surrounded near the north end of Sheep Mountain by neighbors with Winchesters. Several young men hurried out from town to aid in the capture. The man was already dead when they reached the scene of action. He had died, the *Sentinel* reported, from a "dose of powdered opium," self-administered.

There are two versions of what happened next. According to the account which Nye published the following day, the young men from town did not relish the prospect of taking the body to town, which the ranchers expected them to do since they were going that way anyway. One of the young men had a bright idea: He told a false tale about a $750 reward for the body. Thereupon, wrote Nye, a rancher, as expected, snatched the body and started for town at breakneck speed with the jolly townsmen noisily in pursuit. Nye's story said: "It is probably the fastest time ever made by a funeral procession, and the most disgusted man west of the Mississippi went sadly home in the early dawn of that beautiful Sabbath morning, with his one-horse wagon, but no $750."

On the day after Nye's story appeared, an unsigned letter to the editor was published in defense of Motley, the rancher who had brought in the body. The anonymous correspondent said that the men from town arrived three hours after the sheepman died. They had a bottle of whisky and made a general nuisance of themselves. They started for town with the body but when the whisky was gone they wanted to be rid of their burden and persuaded Motley to take over. The rancher, said the letter, had already made promises in town that he would deliver the murderer dead or alive. Moreover, added the correspondent, "the rig was not a one-horse concern."

A few years after he left Laramie, Nye repeated this story with modifications, and called it "Early Day Justice." He said that he saw the body, and "I thought there were signs of ropium, as there was a purple streak around the neck of the deceased, together with other external phenomena not peculiar to opium." He based still another essay, "The Opium Habit," on this incident. Both "Early Day Justice" and "The Opium Habit" are included in this collection. The details in both vary considerably from those given at the time of the killing in 1876.

Nye's seven years in Laramie were busy ones. He went fishing, picnicking, and mining, and participated in all kinds of community affairs. Before twelve months had passed he had not only established a regional reputation for uncommon wit but had also passed the bar (something he had failed to do in Wisconsin), hung out his shingle, begun service as justice, and gotten married. Late in 1877 he dropped his connection with the *Sentinel* and tried to build up his law practice. He was not a howling success. He recalled later that "while I was called Judge Nye, and frequently mentioned in the papers with great consideration, I was out of coal about half the time, and once could not mail my letters for three weeks because I did not have the necessary postage."

While waiting for law clients, Nye wrote paragraphs for the *Laramie Times*, the *Cheyenne Sun*, and the *Denver Tribune*. Then in 1881 he resumed full-time newspaper work as editor of the *Laramie Boomerang*, a new paper which had just been organized by Republican party stalwarts in the community.

Nye published both a daily (peak circulation, three hundred) and a weekly. The front page of the weekly carried the humorous paragraphs collected from the dailies of the previous week. Before long the weekly *Boomerang* was winning readership in far places. Since there are no files of the *Boomerang* in existence for the years 1881–1883, when Nye was editor, the quality of his output for that period has to be judged mainly from his books dating from those years. They are discussed below.

Nye's growing fame and his identification with the dominant wing of the Republican party in Laramie got him an appointment as postmaster in 1882. He delegated the routine responsibilities of his new job, and so did not leave the *Boomerang*.

Nye was finally on the road to financial independence. There is no reason to doubt that he intended to spend the rest of his life in Laramie. But suddenly in November, 1882, he was felled by spinal meningitis. A year of enforced idleness dissipated his savings. Doctors finally advised him that Laramie's 7,200-foot altitude was too much for him, whereupon he severed his connections with the *Boomerang* and the post office, and returned to his boyhood home at Hudson, Wisconsin, just east of Minnesota's Twin Cities.

Fortunately the national reputation that Nye had forged in Laramie survived. As a celebrity he was respected around Hudson, and he spent three quite happy years there. While his health remained precarious, he nevertheless did some excellent writing at a leisurely pace, using mainly themes drawn from his Wyoming recollections. In 1885 the *Boston Globe* began taking a weekly letter from him, and a little later he was hired by the *New York World*. In time sixty other papers were carrying his syndicated column. Also he began lecturing, which in some respects was the worst mistake he ever made, because it cluttered up his life more and more.

Hard winters drove Nye from Wisconsin. After 1886 he was at home in New York City and western North Carolina (near Asheville), but actually he spent little time in either place. In the late 1880's and early 1890's he was the country's best known and best paid humorist, earning $30,000 a year, two thirds of it from lecturing. But he lamented in a personal letter that "fame and belly ache seem to go hand in hand, down through this vale of tears."

Because of chronic illness and overwork, much of what Nye wrote after he left Wyoming and Wisconsin lacked freshness and spontaneity. Whether or not he sensed that his days were numbered, he behaved as if he thought so. He tried to guarantee the security of his wife and children as quickly as possible.

Letters (preserved in the University of Wyoming Library) to his manager, Major James Pond of the Pond Lyceum Bureau, reveal how strenuous his lecture tours were, how often he was sick, and how many times he was on the verge of giving up lecturing. In 1888 he wrote: "If I had a new spine with a cracker on the end of it, I'd lecture over this country till Congress was glad to pay me a big bonus to quit. As it is, I am about ready to state over my signature that this is my farewell tour." An 1889 letter says: "I have told you a thousand times over how uncertain my health has been for six years. You knew it long ago. Now please do not have the idea that I am playing sick or losing several hundred dollars for the excitement of it."

On the tours Nye did not like to furnish a whole evening's entertainment by himself. For four years he traveled with James Whitcomb Riley. The two would take turns on the stage, Nye reciting his humorous essays, and Riley, his poems and stories.

Despite frequent resolutions to give up the exhausting lecture tours, Nye was still making the rounds in 1895. But he had lost his touch and was no longer as amusing as he had been in former years. Tragedy struck at Paterson, New Jersey. He became ill on the platform and could not complete his program. Believing him to be drunk, hoodlums followed him to his train and pelted him with rotten eggs. The story that he had been drunk was reported extensively in the newspapers. This performance at Paterson was his last.

Nye made no public statement but in a private letter he called the drunkenness report "a wicked and cruel lie." His manager also denied the report. Eugene Field and Eli Perkins rose to defend their old friend with the explanation that illness had been mistaken for intoxication. Perkins even wrote to the *Laramie Boomerang* that Nye's physician had given him three teaspoonsful of brandy before the Paterson appearance. Perkins continued: "It struck an empty stomach and a trembling, weak man. The heat of the room, the glare of the foot-lights and the fumes of the slight stimulant overcame him, and he left the platform in a fainting state." About three months after the Paterson incident, Nye suffered a stroke which led to his death ten days later on February 22, 1896, at the age of forty-five. He was buried at Fletcher, North Carolina, near Buck Shoals, which he had called home for the last few years of his life.

It is apparent that rarely after he left Laramie did Nye find conditions favorable for composing humor. On his lecture tours many of his columns had to be turned out on Sunday, leaving him no day of rest. The blighting effect that his lecturing had on his writing did not go unnoticed among discriminating readers. In the spring of 1889 when illness in Nye's family forced him and Riley to interrupt a tour, newspapers thought it just as well. The *Rochester Chronicle*, for example, commented: "Certainly the reputation of neither has been enhanced and the literary work which they have attempted to do in their travels, writing at hotels or on the cars, has been of a character decidedly inferior." When a friend chided him for slipshod writing, Nye replied: "The publishers insist—aye, command me to stand and deliver—and I shall furnish it in quantity regardless of analysis just so long as I am compelled to look the flour barrel, interrogatively, in the face."

Two of Nye's funniest books, *Bill Nye and Boomerang* (1881) and *Forty Liars and Other Lies* (1882), were published before he left Laramie. Their contents consisted mainly of his collected newspaper columns. Before he left for Wisconsin in 1883, Nye clipped the front pages from the office file of the weekly *Boomerang*. He was thus able to take with him the ingredients of *Baled Hay*, which he published in 1884. These three volumes, along with *Remarks by Bill Nye* (1886) contain Nye's best writing. When compiling his *Remarks* in Wisconsin, he drew heavily upon his recollections of life in the West.

All told, Nye's books appeared in fourteen volumes with twenty different titles. He also wrote two plays which were not very well received. Two burlesque histories, one of the United States and one of England, depart from Nye's usual pattern in that they are not collections of short, independent essays. *Bill Nye's History of the United States* (1894) was his best seller, with total sales of 500,000 copies.

His later humor, whether published in newspapers or books, rarely amuses readers of the 1960's. *A Subtreasury of American Humor*, edited by E. B. White and Katharine S. White (New York: Coward-McCann, Inc., © 1941), includes nothing of Nye's. In a section headed "History, Politics, and Affairs of State" the omission is explained as follows: "One of the supposedly humorous American historians was Bill Nye. A chapter from his 'History of the United States' might logically have found a place in here if it had been funny (to us), and we wish it had, because Opper's illustrations are so good." It is true that *Bill Nye's History of the United States*, except for a few sentences here and there, is no longer funny, if it ever was. It seems that by 1894 when he wrote the disappointing *History*, illness and overwork had dried up the wellspring of inspiration. Yet a half million Nye fans bought the book regardless! Perhaps the Frederick Opper illustrations made up to some extent for the shortcomings of the text.

In earlier, happier days in the West, Nye had been really funny. Moreover, to the social historian, Nye's Laramie essays, paragraphs, or columns, whatever we choose to call them, offer a panorama of Western life in the 1870's and 1880's. Nye frequently drew upon his day-to-day experiences, and in so doing recorded accurate details of frontier life. In his attitudes he usually reflected popular Western viewpoints. Indians, braggarts from the East, carpetbagger officials, hypocrites, and frauds of all kinds he despised. His strictures on cowboys who shot up the town probably won the "Amens" of his neighbors. His ridicule of Oscar Wilde, who was lecturing in the U.S. in 1882, dressed in knee breeches, was well received by the man in the street. Even when he scoffed at the agricultural possibilities of Wyoming he had the support of many citizens of Laramie who rejected the excessive claims made by a few promoters. Of course he laughed at himself more than he did at anyone else.

While the attitudes he took were usually calculated to win the approval of his readers, Nye sometimes slashed individuals rather cruelly. Tradition has it that once he had to go into hiding for a

few days at a ranch to avoid physical punishment. He dealt harshly
with his local newspaper competitors, and they retaliated in kind.
Once in giving an account of a party he wrote that Nancy Sherrod,
who was part Indian, was there "painted up like a Shutler
wagon." Nancy's husband took offense at this and was not easily
placated.

Walter Blair in his doctoral dissertation, "The Background of
Bill Nye in American Humor" (Chicago, 1931) shows that many
of Nye's traits, attitudes, and forms were characteristic of various
nineteenth-century writers who preceded him. They had experi-
mented with the devices which Nye adopted. Like them, Nye
wrote burlesques of literary productions, etiquette books,
obituaries, elegant orations, biblical parables, and dramatic
criticisms. Like them, Nye deflated the pompous and debunked
individuals, ideals, and institutions. Like them, he employed puns,
anti-climax, incongruities, exaggeration, homely details, and
absurd foreign phrases. But Nye was able to apply the established
devices to Western materials with a quaint personal touch and
with such skill that he outstripped all of his predecessors in fame
and income.

The selections appearing in this volume have been taken from
Laramie, Cheyenne, and Denver newspapers, and from six books:
Bill Nye and Boomerang (1881), *Forty Liars and Other Lies* (1882),
Baled Hay (1884), *Remarks By Bill Nye* (1886), *Chestnuts* (1887),
and *Nye and Riley's Railway Guide* (1889). All were written in
Laramie, except for some of those taken from *Remarks* and the
two selections from the *Railway Guide*. The selections have been
arranged in roughly chronological order. Dating those taken from
newspapers is no problem, but dating items in books is sometimes
difficult. Nye's usual practice when compiling a book was to dip
into his file of newspaper clippings. He used what he had on hand.
Perhaps he added a few fresh items that had not appeared in
newspapers. This makes it possible to assign most of his material
pretty definitely to particular years, but in some cases internal
evidence indicates that essays were not put in books until years
after their first appearance in newspapers. At any rate, an effort
has been made to place the selections in the order in which they
were written. The selections have been reprinted exactly as they

appeared in the original except for the correction of obvious misprints and except for a few omissions, indicated by three dots, in excessively long essays. Editorial interpolations have been enclosed in brackets.

Tastes in humor have changed in the seventy years since Bill Nye died, but much that he wrote still transmits to the contemporary reader the whimsy and the idiocy that make people laugh. In addition, it is of value to the social historian since it pictures frontier customs and characters and illuminates the popular taste of the 1880's and 1890's.

T. A. LARSON

Laramie, Wyoming

Bibliographical Note

He who would learn more about Bill Nye's life may well begin by reading *Bill Nye: His Own Life Story*, with continuity by the humorist's son, Frank Wilson Nye (New York: The Century Co., 1926). To pursue the study of Nye's place in American humor one should read Walter Blair's doctoral dissertation, "The Background of Bill Nye in American Humor" (University of Chicago, 1931), and his *Native American Humor, 1800–1900* (New York: American Book Co., 1937, and San Francisco: Chandler Pub. Co., 1960).

The collection of Nye's letters to Major James Pond of the Pond Lyceum Bureau, in the University of Wyoming Library, are valuable for their details of the humorist's experiences on his lecture tours. Pond quoted from a few of these letters in dealing with Nye in his book, *Eccentricities of Genius* (New York: Dillingham, 1900). A small gathering of other letters by Nye has been edited by N. Orwin Rush, *Letters of Edgar Wilson Nye* (Laramie: University of Wyoming Library, 1950). The docket book in which Nye recorded his business as justice of the peace during the years 1877–1882 is preserved in the University of Wyoming Library. Other significant manuscript holdings are at the University of California, Los Angeles, the University of North Carolina, and the Wisconsin State Historical Society. The only known issues of Nye's newspaper, *The Boomerang*, are two preserved in the University of Wyoming Library. They contain no Nye humor. The *New York World*, which carried long Nye columns regularly on Sundays, 1887–1895, is available in the New York Public Library. The *Denver Tribune*, which published many Nye columns in 1880, is available in Denver at the State Historical Society of Colorado.

For insights into various phases of Nye's career a helpful little book is one edited by Frank Thompson Searight, *The American Press Humorists' Book*, "Bill Nye" monument edition (Los Angeles: edited and published by Frank Thompson Searight at the plant of the *West Coast Magazine*, 1907). Included in this scarce volume are comments by James Barton Adams, M. C. Barrow (Bill Barlow), and John B. Elliott. William L. Visscher's *Ten Wise Men and Some More* (Chicago: Press Club, privately printed, 1909) includes material on Nye, as does Melville D. Langdon's *Kings of the Platform and Pulpit* (Chicago, 1891).

The volume by Marcus Dickey, *The Maturity of James Whitcomb Riley* (Indianapolis: Bobbs-Merrill, 1922) treats Riley's relations with Nye, but was written without the aid of the Nye letters to Major Pond mentioned above.

The following articles are also recommended:

Walter Blair, "Burlesques in Nineteenth-Century American Humorists," *American Literature*, II (1930), 236–247.

W. E. Chaplin, "Bill Nye," *Frontier*, XI (1931), 223–226.
[Chaplin worked with Nye on the *Boomerang* in Laramie.]

———, "Recollections of Bill Nye," published in the *Laramie Republican*, February 24, 1896.

Levette J. Davidson, "Bill Nye and *The Denver Tribune*," *The Colorado Magazine*, IV (January, 1928), 13–18.

Edmund H. Eitel, "Letters of Riley and Bill Nye," *Harpers Monthly Magazine*, CXXXVIII (1919), 473–484.

T. A. Larson, "Laramie's Bill Nye," *1952 Brand Book* (Denver: Denver Westerners, 1953), pp. 35–56.

Walt McDougall, "Pictures in the Papers," *American Mercury*, VI (September, 1925), 67–73.
[McDougall did illustrations for Nye on the *New York World*.]

Don C. Seitz, "The Last of the Old School," *The Literary Review*, VII (1926), 1.

Edgar Watson, "Bill Nye's Experience," *Annals of Wyoming*, XVI (1944), 65–70.

Contents

INTRODUCTION   v

BIBLIOGRAPHICAL NOTE   xv

LIST OF ILLUSTRATIONS   xxi

SELECTIONS FROM BILL NYE

Puff	1
How Great Men Dance	3
Nye's New Second Reader	5
The Old, Old Story	7
Nye's Comments After a Jail Break	8
Drawbacks of Public Life	9
The Annual Wail	11
The Great Rocky Mountain Reunion of Yaller Dogs	13
Clams vs Indians	15
The Great, Horrid Man Receiveth New Year Calls	17
A Territorial Secretary	19
A General Opinion of a Wilhelmj Concert	21
Mining Stampedes and Their Symptoms	23
Wyoming Farms, Etc., Etc.	26
The Parable of the Prodigal Son	28
Catching Mountain Trout at an Elevation of 8000 Feet	31
The Same Old Thing	33
Examining the Brand of a Frozen Steer	36
Fine-Cut as a Means of Grace	37
My Mine	39
The Nocturnal Cow	41

Apostrophe to an Orphan Mule   43
Hong Lee's Grand Benefit at Leadville   45
The Rocky Mountain Hog   47
The Temperature of the Bumble-Bee   49
Suggestions for a School of Journalism   50
The Buckness Wherewith the Buck Beer Bucketh   54
The Lop-Eared Lovers of the Little Laramie   55
Queer   61
The Weather and Some Other Things   62
Some Thoughts on Childhood   63
A Christmas Ride in July   65
The Gentle Youth from Leadville   66
Home-Made Indian Relics   68
Circular from Colorow   70
The Plug Hat in Wyoming   72
How They Salt a Claim   74
Women Wanted   76
A Headlight in View   79
Our Compliments   82
Mania for Marking Clothes   83
The Woes of a One-Legged Man   85
The Woman with the Hose   88
Table Etiquette   90
The Female Barber   92
A Word About Wild Sheep   93
Bill Nye's Complaint   95
Entomologist   96
Wilting a Lion   99
Obituary for Captain Jack   102
The Stage Bald-Head   104
Apostrophe Addressed to O. Wilde   106
The Western "Chap"   108
Accepting the Laramie Postoffice   110
A Fire at a Ball   111
Fruit   112
The Mimic Stage   113
Greeley and Rum   116
Household Recipes   118

The Codfish   120
Table Manners of Children   122
Catching a Buffalo   124
The Church Debt   127
Done It A-Purpose   130
One Kind of Fool   134
Picnic Incidents   136
The Duke of Rawhide   139
A Resign   141
Squaw Jim   144
Man Overbored   146
The Cow-Boy   149
Early Day Justice   152
My Dog   155
Rev. Mr. Hallelujah's Hoss   157
A Father's Letter   159
Taxidermy   161
Petticoats at the Polls   164
The Opium Habit   167
A Father's Advice to His Son   169
A Mountain Snowstorm   172
Her Tired Hands   175
Where He First Met His Parents   180
No More Frontier   182

List of Illustrations

Sketch of Bill Nye   Frontispiece

The Indian Girl of Story and of Fact   *Facing page* 11

The Mania for Marking Clothes   *Facing page* 83

The Mimic Stage   *Facing page* 113

An Unequal Match   *Facing page* 124

Charcoal Brown's Reproaches   *Facing page* 136

The Duke of Rawhide   *Facing page* 139

Nye and a Farmer   *Facing page* 175

Nye Contemplating His Birthplace   *Facing page* 180

All illustrations from the collection of the editor

Bill Nye's
Western Humor

Puff

The newspaper puff is something which makes you feel bad if you don't get it. The groundwork for a newspaper puff consists of a good, moral character and a good bank account. Writing newspaper puffs is like mixing sherry cobblers and mint juleps all through the summer months, for customers, and quenching your own thirst with rain water.

Sometimes a man is looking for a puff and don't get it; then he says that the paper is going down hill, and that it is in the hands of a monopoly, and he would stop the paper if he didn't have to pay his bill first.

Writing a newspaper puff is like taking a photograph of a homely baby. If the photograph doesn't represent the child as resembling a beautiful cherub with wings, and halos, and harps, and things, it shows that the artist does not understand his business. So it is with a newspaper puff—if the puffee don't stand out like the bold and fearless exponent of truth and morality, it shows that the puffer doesn't understand human nature.

It is more fun to watch a man read a puff of himself than it is to see a fat man slip up on an orange peel. The narrow-minded man reads it over seven or eight times, and then goes around to the different places in town where the paper is taken, and steals what copies he can. The kind-hearted family man goes home and reads it to his wife, and then pays up his bill on the paper. The successful business man, who advertises and makes money, starts immediately to find the newspaper man and speak a word of grateful acknowledgment and encouragement. Then the two men start out of the sanctum and walk thoughtfully down the street together, and the successful business man takes sugar in his, and the newspaper man doesn't put anything in his, and then they

1

both eat a clove or two, and life is pleasanter and sweeter, and peace settles down like a turtle dove in their hearts, and after awhile lamp-posts get more plenty, and everybody seems to be more or less intoxicated, but the hearts of these two men are filled with a nameless joy, because they know just where to stop, and not make themselves ridiculous.

From *Laramie Daily Sentinel*, January 6, 1877.

How Great Men Dance

An exchange says that: "Mr. Sartoris, now in Washington, dances in such a horribly muscular, awkward and dangerous manner, that Nellie almost wishes that she had not married him." This leads us to say that great men are not, as a rule, noted for their swan-like movements in the dreamy dance. We are sorry to acknowledge that we are not an exception to the rule. In fact, the more genius a man has, the more successful he is as a circus and ten allied shows in one when he undertakes to dance. The truly great man goes into a quadrille with the same zeal and evident relish that the average editor manifests at the funeral of a newspaper thief, or while reading the inscription on a tombstone reared by loving hands over the man, who, during life, stole his jokes. He cannot disguise his interest in the game, like old veteran dancers. He swings his partner with such wonderful zeal that her feet stand out at an angle of 45 degrees with the centrifugal force. In the grand right and left, he eagerly catches hold of the first lady he comes across, and swings her around by the thumb seven or eight times in his original and beautiful style. He seems to throw his whole soul into the business, and dances like a hired man. He doesn't seem to notice that all the occupants of the ball room are neglecting their own dances and engaging reserved seats to watch his grand and lofty tumbling.

In the Lancers, when the "side four separate," he seems to labor under the impression that he ought to separate and dance a little on both sides to avoid being called partial or prejudiced, but after a while gives it up as a physiological impossibility, picks out a good train to step on, leaps gracefully from that one to another one, and then stops to get his breath.

Then he looks around the hall for some applause, but is most always disappointed. Between dances he goes off into a dressing room, ostensibly to get a drink of water, but in reality to sew on some suspender buttons and spit on his hands.

At the first of the evening his programme looms up first-rate, but in an hour or two there are left only a few brave girls who want to go into partnership and watch him play "leap frog" or "pom pom pullaway" to fast music. None but the ladies with strong nerves care to be in the same set, and run the risk of having their front teeth knocked out when he turns hand-springs and double sommersaults, under the delusion that it is a balance or a promenade or something of that nature.

If you want to see a genuine panic in a ball room, turn a great man loose, and see him waltz like the baby elephant and promenade like the Suffolk hog going to war. He prances "up and down the center" like a guinea pig that is "cursed with an inward pain," and winds up the evening performance by trying to dance a heel and toe polka. He gives his partner the advantage of the "under hold," but she throws up the sponge just as he is getting interested. She accuses him of being drunk, and he is delighted to think how he has fooled her. He is only too happy to be considered drunk, if people will forgive him for dancing like a Ute brave with low necked clothes on. He buries his secret in his breast, and chuckles inwardly over the fact that people attribute his poor dancing to drunkenness. But away down in his heart, where nobody can see, there is a blessed assurance which buoys him up in the years to come. It is a pleasure that the world cannot give nor take away, and it is this—he knows that he wasn't drunk.

From *Laramie Daily Sentinel*, January 7, 1877.

Nye's New Second Reader

O come, boys and girls and see the young folks skate. Can you skate? Skating is fine sport for those who can skate right side up. Once there was a young man who tried to skate over an air-hole, but he didn't come home when dinner was ready, and he hasn't got back yet. Some people think that he skated into an air-hole and died. There isn't so much air in an air-hole as the name seems to imply. People who skate into air-holes ought to leave word before hand that they will not be back in time for dinner. Then if the mashed potatoes and string beans get cold, it's nobody's business.

Once there was a little boy, with long, yellow hair and cheeks, and dimpled eyebrows, who went to skate on a mill-pond, but he had a large Newfoundland dog that went with him. The sun shone brightly, and all along the street little boys were preparing to celebrate the Fourth of July, and go in swimming. But the dog clung to his young master, wagging his large, mournful tail in the summer air as he trotted along toward the smooth ice where the boy was to skate all the forenoon, for it was Monday morning, because his mother was washing on Monday forenoons, and had cold dinners. There may not be any visible connection between these two, but it was his rule to skate on Monday forenoon anyhow, the year round.

Well, he had skated in this way for two hours, alone, with the exception of the large dog, that was watching the little boy's coat and luncheon, when the ice gave a great crack and the little boy was not to be seen. His little cap spun around in the whirling cold waters a few times, and at last went out of sight. But the dog saw it all at a glance. He saw the wild rush of the cruel waters as they closed over the long yellow hair, and consigned the little idol of his parents to the cold, dark bosom of the river. Then the large Newfoundland dog rose up and picked the mince pie out of the little boy's lunch and ate it. After he ate it he happened to think that in cases of that kind it was customary for large Newfoundland dogs to take off their clothes and go in and rescue the little boys, but he didn't think of it in time. He atoned for it though by mourning over the little boy's grave, for weeks and weeks refused to be comforted, or to take any nourishment—except mince pie, and at last he stretched himself out on the little boy's grave and died, on a golden Indian Summer day in autumn—of dyspepsia.

Moral:—Always be kind to the poor.

From *Laramie Daily Sentinel*, February 7, 1877.

The Old, Old Story

Last evening a man who was riding a mule along Fourth street, noticed that the animal walked a little lame; so he alighted, and, resting the mule's gambrel on his shoulder, he took a long, tin spectacle case out of his pocket, and, adjusting his glasses, proceeded to examine the animal's hoof with great care. We called round at the man's residence early this morning to see how he was getting along. The doctor wouldn't allow him to talk much, on account of his fractured jaw, but we learned from his broken conversation that just as he had discovered that a large assortment of Chinese fireworks and Roman candles had worked in under the frog of the mule's foot, he found himself over in the court house yard, picking pieces of spectacles out of his face. The Doctor says that he thinks he can save the third and fourth joints of the neck, but the man will always have to wear a cork head and false face. This is just as it should be, for men who persist in looking into the behindest foot of a mule should always wear cork heads. It is very appropriate that they should.

From *Laramie Daily Sentinel*, February 16, 1877.

Nye's Comments After a Jail Break

Different rumors pervaded the town last evening between the hours of 8 p.m. and 10. Some had understood that the jailor had been struck in the cerebellum, others that he was struck in the act of locking the iron gate. It was earnestly reported at one time that the court house had been surrounded by a large Russian force, and that some were rushin' in and others rushin' out. Great alarms were manifested on the street. Potatoes went up to four cents a pound and everybody went up to the court house. Random shots were heard occasionally on the outskirts of town, and ever and anon a solitary horseman would be seen wending his way; women went through the streets looking wildly in Wagner's and Abbott's and hastily scanning the spring calicoes; grocers insanely presented unreceipted bills to their customers, and customers tore them up in their frenzy; wild-eyed men rushed into saloons and quaffed the flowing bowl, forgetting to pay, and for a time a scene of dismay and panic was to be seen everywhere. Two hundred and eleven women looked under two hundred and eleven beds before retiring, and the man of the house put his trusty Smith and Wesson under his pillow where it wouldn't be stolen. During the still hours of the night he would feel that he must shoot somebody, and as a slight noise greeted his ear he would creep to the door and shoot a hole in the rain-water barrel.

From *Laramie Daily Sentinel*, June 1, 1877.

Drawbacks of Public Life

I always like to tell anything that has the general effect of turning the laugh on me, because then I know there will be no hard feelings. It is very difficult to select any one who will stand publicity when that publicity is more amusing to the average reader than to the chief actor. Every little while I run out of men who enjoy being written about in my chaste and cheerful vein. Then I have to come forward and take this position myself. It is not egotism, as some might suppose. It is unselfishness and a manly feeling of self-sacrifice.

Last year I consented to read the Declaration of Independence, as my share of the programme, partially out of gallantry toward the Goddess of Liberty, and partly to get a ride with the chaplain and orator of the day, through the principal streets behind the band. It was a very proud moment for me. I felt as though I was holding up one corner of the national fabric myself, and I naturally experienced a pardonable pride about it. I sat in the carriage with the compiled laws of Wyoming under my arm, and looked like Daniel Webster wrapped in a large bale of holy calm. At the grounds I found that most everybody was on the speakers' stand, and the audience was represented by a helpless and unhappy minority.

At a Fourth of July celebration it is wonderful how many great men there are, and how they swarm on the speakers' platform. Then there are generally about thirteen venerable gentlemen who do not pretend to be great, but they cannot hear very well, so they get on the speakers' stand to hear the same blood-curdling statements that they have heard for a thousand years. While I was reading the little burst of humor known as the Declaration, the staging gave way under the accumulated weight of the Fourth

Infantry band and several hundred great men who had invited themselves to sit on the platform. The Chaplain fell on top of me, and the orator of the day on top of him. A pitcher of ice water tipped over on me, and the water ran down my back. A piece of scantling and an alto horn took me across the cerebellum, and as often as I tried to get up and throw off the Chaplain and orator of the day and Fourth Infantry band, the greased pig which had been shut up under the stand temporarily, would run between my legs and throw me down again. I never knew the reading of the Declaration of Independence to have such a telling effect. I went home without witnessing the closing exercises. I did not ride home in the carriage. I told the committee that some poor, decrepit old woman might ride home in my place. I needed exercise and an opportunity to commune with myself.

As I walked home by an unfrequented way, I thought of the growth and grandeur of the republic, and how I could get rid of the lard that had been wiped on my clothes by the oleaginous pig. This year, when the committee asked me to read the Declaration, I said pleasantly but firmly that I would probably be busy on that day soaking my head, and therefore would have to decline.

From *Bill Nye and Boomerang*.

THE INDIAN GIRL OF STORY.   THE INDIAN GIRL OF FACT.

The Indian Girl of Story and of Fact by Fred Opper

The Annual Wail

As usual, the regular fall wail of the eastern press on the Indian question, charging that the Indians never commit any depredations unless grossly abused, has arrived. We are unpacking it this morning and marking the price on it. Some of it is on manifold and the remainder on ordinary telegraph paper. It will be closed out very cheap. Parties wishing to supply boarding schools with essays and compositions cannot do better than to apply at once. We are selling Boston lots, with large brass-mounted words, at two and three cents per pound. Every package draws a prize of a two-pound can of baked beans. If large orders are received from any one person, we will set up the wail and start it to running, free of cost. It may be attached to any newspaper in a few minutes, and the merest child can readily understand it. It is very simple. But it is not as simple as the tallowy poultice on the average eastern paper, who grinds them out at $4 per week, and found.

We also have some old wails, two or three years old—and older —that have never been used, which we will sell very low. Old Sioux wails, Modoc wails, etc., etc. They do not seem to meet with a ready sale in the west, and we rather suspect it's because we are too near the scene of the Indian troubles. Parties who have been shot at, scalped, or had their wives and children massacred by the Indians, do not buy eastern wails. Eastern wails are meant for the eastern market, and if we can get this old stock off our hands, we will hereafter treat the Indian question in our own plain, matter of fact way.

The namby pamby style of Indian editorial and molasses candy gush that New Englanders are now taking in, makes us tired. Life is too short. It is but a span. Only as a tale that has been told. Just like the coming of a guest, who gets his meal ticket punched, grabs a tooth pick, and skins out.

11

Then why do we fool away the golden years that the Creator has given us for mental improvement and spiritual elevation, in trying to fill up the enlightened masses with an inferior article of taffy?

Every man who knows enough to feed himself out of a maple trough, knows, or ought to know, that the Indian is treacherous, dishonest, diabolical, and devilish in the extreme, and that he is only waiting the opportunity to spread out a little juvenile Hell over the fair face of nature if you give him one sixteenth of a chance. He will wear pants and comb his hair and pray and be a class leader at the Agency for 59 years, if he knows that in the summer of the 60th year he can murder a few Colorado settlers and beat out the brains of the industrious farmers.

Industry is the foe of the red man. He is a warrior. He has royal blood in his veins, and the vermin of the Montezumas dance the German over his filthy carcass. That's the kind of hair pin he is. He never works. Nobody but Chinamen and plebians ever work.

But we will desist. Every time we tackle this matter, we get so excited that we say too much. We are not belligerent or inclined to be captious, but O how we yearn for a stuffed club and sufficient leisure to go into the sanctums of these North American pack animals and wallop their systems into prepared dog meat. We speak of these Indian editorial writers as pack animals because that is the term that may safely be used in the presence of ladies, but that is not what we mean. No indeed. We call on the great civilized world to witness that that is not what we mean.

From *Cheyenne Daily Sun*, October 7, 1879; reprinted from *Laramie Times*.

The Great Rocky Mountain
Reunion of Yaller Dogs

Secretary Spates, the silver-tongued orator and gilt-edged mouth organ of Wyoming, acting general superintendent and governor extraordinary of Wyoming, expressed a wish the other day for a dog. He had a light yellow cane, and wanted a dog to match. He said that he wanted something to love. If he could wake up in the stillness of the night and hear his faithful dog fighting fleas, and licking his chops, and coughing, he (the secretary) would feel as though he was beloved, at least, by one. Some friends thought it would be a pleasant thing to surprise Mr. Spates with a dog. So they procured a duplicate key to his room and organized themselves into a dog vigilance committee. There were several yellow dogs around Cheyenne that were not in use, and their owners consented to part with them and try to control their grief while they worried along from day to day without them. These dogs were collected and placed in the secretary's room.

Throwing a heterogeneous mass of dogs together in that way, and all of them total strangers to each other, in the natural course of things creates something of a disturbance, and that was the result in this case. When the secretary arrived, the dogs were holding a session with closed doors. The presiding officer had lost control, and a surging crowd of yellow dogs had the floor. Only one dog was excepted. He was struggling with all his strength against the most colossal attack of colic that ever convulsed a pale, yellow dog. Just as he would get to feeling kind of comfortable, a spasm would catch him on the starboard quarter and his back would hump itself like a 1,000-legged worm, and with such force as to thump the floor with the stumpy tail of the demoralized dog and jar the bric-a-brac on the brackets and what-nots of the Secretary of Wyoming Territory.

Just then the secretary arrived. He was whistling a trill or two from the "Turkish Patrol," when he got within earshot of the convention. Several people met him and asked him what was going on up in his room. The secretary blushed and said he guessed there was nothing out of character, and wondered if someone was putting up a Conkling story on him, to kill a Spates boom.

When he got to the door and went in, thirty-seven dogs ran between his legs, and went out the door with a good deal of intensity. More of them would have run between the secretary's legs, but they couldn't all make it.

Mr. Spates was mad. He felt hurt and grieved. The dogs had jumped on the bed and torn the pillow shams into minute bandages, and wiped their feet on the coverlid. They had licked the blacking off his boots, and eaten his toilet soap. One of them had tried on the secretary's dressing gown; but it was not large enough, and he had taken it off in a good deal of a hurry.

Long after it was supposed that the last dog had gone out, yellow dogs, of different degrees of yellowishness, and moving in irregular orbits, would be thrown from the secretary's room with great force. Some of them were killed, while others were painfully injured. It is said that there are fewer yellow dogs in Cheyenne now than there used to be, and those that are there are more subdued, and reserved, and taciturn, and skinned on the back, than they used to be; while the secretary has a far-away look in his eye, like a man who has trusted humanity once too often, and been everlastingly and unanimously left.

From *Bill Nye and Boomerang*.

Clams vs Indians

In another article in this issue is given the former residence and occupation of those who are immediately connected with the Indian management. It will be seen that they are, almost without exception, from the Atlantic coast, where they have had about the same opportunity to become acquainted with the duties pertaining to their appointment as Lucifer has had for the past two thousand years to form a warm personal acquaintance with the prophet Isaiah.

With all due respect to the worthy descendants of the Pilgrim Fathers, and not wishing to cast a slur upon the ability or the integrity of the dwellers along the rock-bound coast of New England, we will say in the mildest manner possible that these men are no more fit to manage hostile Indians than Perdition is naturally fitted for a powder house.

A man may successfully cope with the wild and fierce codfish in his native jungle or beard the salt water clam in his den, and still signally fail as an Indian agent. The Codfish is not treacherous. He may be bold, blood-thirsty and terrible, but he will never go back on a treaty. Who ever heard of a codfish going back on his word? Who ever heard of a codfish leaving the reservation and spreading desolation over the land? No one. The expression on the face of a codfish shows that he is perfectly open and above board.

We might say the same of the clam. Of course if driven to the wall, as it were, he will fight; but we have yet to find a single instance in the annals of history where the clam—unless grossly insulted and openly put upon—ever made an open out-break.

This is why we claim that clam culture and Indian management are not analagous. They are not simultaneous nor co-extensive. They are not identical or homogeneous.

We feel that in treating this subject in our candid and truthful way, perhaps the Administration will not feel hurt and grieved; but if they do, we can't help it. The great reading public seems to look to us, as much as to say: "What are your views on this great subject which is agitating the public mind?" We can't evade it, and even if President Hayes were our own brother instead of being a warm personal friend and admirer of ours, we would certainly speak right out as we have spoken out and tell the whole broad Republic of Columbia that to successfully steer a hostile tribe of nervous, refractory and irritable Indian bummers past the rocks and shoals of war is one thing, and to drive a salt water clam up a hickory tree and kill him with a club, is entirely another thing.

From *Cheyenne Daily Sun*, October 17, 1879; reprinted from *Laramie Times*.

The Great, Horrid Man
Receiveth New Year Calls

In my Boudoir, Dec. 20, 1879.

New Year's Day will be Leap Year, and the ladies want to make calls.

The masculine man will, therefore, have to receive. Some of us will club together at private houses and receive, while others will "hire a hall" and sling a great deal of agony, no doubt. I shall be at home to some extent. I shall wear my organdy, looped up with demi-overskirt of the same, and three-ply lambrequins of Swiss, with corded edges and button-holes of elephant's breath cut plain. My panier is down at the machine shop now and will be done in a few days. I shall be assisted by Superintendent Dickinson and First Assistant Postmaster General Spalding of the Laramie postoffice department, and the grand difficulty will no doubt occur at the residence of the latter.

Mr. Dickinson will wear a lavender *moire antique* with all wool underclothes. The costume will be draped on the side with bevel pinions, and looped back with English button-holes, and cut low in the neck.

Mr. Spalding will wear a cream-colored walking suit with train No. 4. He will also wear buttons with button-holes to match. Sleeves cut Princesse, with polished elbows of same. Boots plain with cranberry sauce. Brocaded silk overskirt, with lemon sauce. Fifty-three button kids, fastening to the suspenders, open back, with Italian dressing.

I give these notes to the reporter in advance, because women are so apt to get these things all mixed up. After we have spent so much time constructing an elaborate wardrobe, we do not wish the journals of the Territory to come out the next day, and make each one of us appear like "a perfect dud." Our table will also look the nicest of any in town. We have designed it ourselves. We have arranged the hose so that we can play it on the dishes after we have used them, and save splashing around in hot water between meals. We intend to feed the first three or four delegations without doing any work on the dishes. Visitors will be made to feel perfectly at home. Callers will be required not to spit on the floor. Parties making calls will not be allowed to throw peanut shells in the card-receiver, or leave their muddy articles on the piano. Callers will please remain seated while the frigid sustenance is circulated. No standing callers allowed. Standing collars are going out of style anyhow.

From *Bill Nye and Boomerang.*

A Territorial Secretary

Laramie City, Jan. 8. Perhaps it is wrong to speak lightly of the absent and smile at the misfortunes of those whose intellects are a little out of plumb, but I cannot ignore the man who, during his short official career in Wyoming, has most sought for newspaper prominence. Secretary A. Worth Spates, who has for less than a year formed one of the prominent features of a grand, gloomy and terrific Territorial administration, is now in Washington, D.C., as many of the readers of *The Tribune* already know. He is not there on Territorial business, nor to visit his family. He did not go to the capital at this season of the year on account of his health. He is there more particularly to ask for executive clemency.

It seems that the President, taking advantage of his high position, and "clothed in a little brief authority," has nominated a new Secretary for Wyoming, thus intimating to Mr. Spates that the ponderous machinery of government will try to worry along some way without him. Although the brainy Secretary has it in his head that he is the motive power, the fly wheel and chronometer balance of the great political engine, a failure on the part of certain parties at Washington to grapple with this truth is likely to ship-wreck the life of one whose only failing has been that he loved the people of Wyoming too well.

I do not wish to be understood as hostile to the Secretary, for I am not. He has never harmed me by word or deed. But as a citizen of Wyoming I hate to be imposed upon. I came here to build up the Territory and develop its resources. My idea was to make the plains of Wyoming blossom as the rose. It is, however, up-hill work to advance the interests of the embryo State unless I have the co-operation of The Government.

No man, single-handed, can pave the way for wealth and enlightenment, when every two weeks a reclaimed lunatic or star idiot is sent here to get a square meal and give away the affairs of State to all eternity. At times I am free to say that I am discouraged and disheartened.

Dealing with a particular class of fools is easy enough, because you get used to their ways, but when a minister plenipotentiary is busy at all seasons of the year ransacking the globe to secure rare and costly specimens of new and unique fools, it becomes a difficult task even to catalogue and arrange them.

Mr. Spates will ever remain green in the memory of his constituents. The reason for this will be perfectly plain to the thinking mind. He will be remembered as the champion intellectual light weight of his time. He will stand out on the pages of some future cyclopedia as the man with the go-as-you-please appetite and the angle worm legs. But let us hope that he will not disappear from our view, even though he may be removed from office. Wherever he goes he will not be lost. Nothing is lost in the great economy of nature. No matter how small an infinitesimal atom it may be it will not be sufficient to drop out of existence. In the great store house of nature these little particles are filed away and in the glad morning of the eventful future this atom, floating about in the winter atmosphere of Washington, will appear perhaps as a molecule or animalcula, or it may bloom in the daisy or ripen in the gentle nodding pumpkin blossom, or it may work its way up the scale of animal progression and come to the front as a potato bug or some other warbler of the woods. No, kind indulgent reader, he will not be lost. He may get terribly bewildered, and there may be two or three search warrants, and a reward and a microscope out after him at times, but he will always be found. That is why a temporary feeling of gloom and sorrow oppresses me as I write these lines.

From *Denver Tribune*, January 11, 1880.

A General Opinion of a Wilhelmj Concert

Laramie City, Wyo., March 13, 1880. On Monday evening last at this place Wilhelmj was well received, there being about all that Blackburn's hall could comfortably hold at $1.00 and $1.25 per head. Laramie, for a town of her size, is immensely enthusiastic over all kinds of musical entertainments, and starved out as she has been for a long time, the simple intimation of something new to her people brings out a large and generally appreciative audience.

Unfortunately we haven't people enough to expect the highest order of talent generally, and our opera house being a little cramped for space, and the scenery and stage being a little meagre for large dramatic companies, and situated as we are about midway between Omaha and Ogden, with few towns of any size along the road, the smaller companies hate to pay so much fare in order to reach us. We, therefore, generally get those only who try to reach 'Frisco, and get busted at this point. In this way our hotel men have collected a large number of dramatic wardrobes, which they now hold in solution to apply on board.

Through the enterprise of Mr. Blackburn the Wilhelmj concert was secured, and we hope during another year to receive the attention of musical troupes to which we are fully entitled.

Herr Wilhelmj seems to get a good deal of melody out of a violin. Many of our young men who have been learning to play the violin and had adjourned, will now open out again. This is one reason why I regret that Wilhelmj stopped off here.

But if you have a piano that has got bilious and unhappy and misanthropical, and don't seem to care for life, Mr. Vogrich is the

21

man to stir it up and open its pores and knock the supreme saw-dust out of it.

Vog. don't look like a man who would stir up the true inward-ness of a piano that way. He comes forward to the footlights, bows till his fair soft hair hangs over his features and gets into his eyes, and he looks like one who simply wants to be loved. He then sits down to the instrument and plays two or three low throbs of melody. After he finishes up the throb contract, he throws in about eleven aspijios to kind of mop off the dust and get himself mad. He then throws her wide open and gives her sand. Monday evening he played Somnambula. It is a little Fantasie that old man Liszt dashed off one morning before breakfast. It starts off with a wild tremulous wail like that of the man who rises in the stilly night to get a glass of water for some loved one and falls over the oleander and upsets the aquarium into the easy chair.

Then it widens and deepens till it gathers power and the indica-tor shows a pressure of about 200 pounds and he puts in a strain where the composer imagines himself in a boiler factory. So perfect is the imitation that one can almost hear the grunt of the man who wields the hammer.

Marie Salvotti does not play the piano. She sings. She sang L'estassi. She also asked a young man to meet her several times but he didn't seem to meet her with a great deal of assiduity. She therefore kept insisting on it and seemed to get a good deal excited. I don't know why he didn't meet her for he certainly must have heard her. He might have been delayed by a washout on the C.P. road. Her voice seems to have a large compass. There is an Alpine scene at the back of the stage and Marie seemed so irritated be-cause the young man didn't meet her on schedule time that she gave a war whoop that knocked Mr. Vogrich clear over the piano, and a tie chopper or something of that kind came out of the brush about half way up the side of the Alps and wanted to know what in the name of General Jackson and the Continental Congress was the matter. I only give this to show what a range of voice Marie has when she turns herself loose.

From *Denver Tribune*, March 16, 1880.

Mining Stampedes and Their Symptoms

Aside from these little ripples on the current of our metropolitan life we have on the average about two

MINING STAMPEDES

per day when the weather is good.

Symptom 1.—A long-haired man is seen pounding up a piece of quartz about the size of a man's hand.

Symptom 2.—Two men meander up to him and ask him where he got it.

Symptom 3.—The long-haired man looks down into the mortar and lies gently to the inquiring minds who linger near.

Symptom 4.—More men come around. The long-haired man gets a gold-pan and doubles himself up over the ditch and begins to pan.

Symptom 5.—Two hundred more men come out of saloons and other mercantile establishments and join the throng.

Symptom 6.—The long-haired man gets down to black sand, and shows several colors about the size of a blue-jay's ear.

Symptom 7.—Several solitary horsemen start out, with some pack-mules and blank location notices and valley tan. The plot deepens. The telegraph gets red hot. Men who have been impecunious for lo these many years, come around to pay some old bills. Poor men buy spotted dogs and gold-headed canes. Stingy men get reckless and buy the first box of strawberries without asking the price.

I have caught the epidemic myself.

I am getting reckless. Instead of turning my last-summer lavender pants behind side before, and removing the ham-sandwich lithograph on the front breadths, I have purchased a new pair.

I never experienced such a wild, glad feeling of perfect abandon.

I go to church and chip in for the heathen perfectly regardless of expense. If Zion languishes, I come forward and throw in the small currency with a lavish hand.

Banks, offices, hotels, saloons and private residences show specimens of quartz carrying free gold and carbonates, hard, soft and medium soft, with iron protoxide of nitrogen, rhombohedral glucose indication of valedictory and free milling oxide of antifat in abundance.

Nellis, who lives near the Mill creek carbonate claims, came in to town the other day to get an injunction against the miners, so that he could injunct them from prospecting in his cellar and staking his pie-plant bed.

When he goes out after dark to drive the cow out of his turnip patch, he falls over a stake every little while, with a notice tacked on it which sets forth that the undersigned, viz., Johnny Comelately, Joe Newbegin, Shoo Fly Smith and Union Forever Dandelion claim 1,500 feet in length by 600 feet in width for mineral purposes on this claim, to be known as "The Gal with the Skim milk Eye," together with all dips, spurs, angles or variations, solid silver or other precious metals therein contained.

Mr. Nellis says he is glad to see a "boom," and at first he did all he could to make it pleasant for prospectors, but lately he thinks that their sociability has become too earnest and too simultaneous.

I told him that the only way I could see to avoid losing his grip and having his string beans dug up prematurely was to strike the entire ranch as a placer claim, buy him a Gatling gun that would shoot the large size of buckshot, and then trust in the mysterious movements of an overwhelming Providence.

I do not know whether he took my advice or not, but I am looking anxiously along the Mill creek road every day for a six mule team loaded with disorganized remains, and driven by a man who looks as though he had glutted his vengeance, and had two or three gluts left over on his hands.

I do not, of course, wish to state anything whatever that the circumstances will not bear me out in, for I have worked patiently for many years to build up the enviable reputation for square-toed veracity which I now have, and I cannot afford to fool it away, but I would be glad to see this thing turn out as it bids fair to do.

I have a small lot here in Sherrod's addition to Laramie City, which I would like to sell at a large advance on the first cost. There is a fine deposit of alkali on it, also a mortgage. There are all the improvements that I have put on the property since I bought it, but I would throw in some prairie dogs and other personal property with the lot.

It is pleasantly located, facing toward the center and has an old circus ring on it. It is also so arranged that it catches a good many old beer bottles, pickle bottles, oyster cans, umbrellas, stove pipe and old iron. In a good year I can catch enough old iron on that property to buy a tin milk pan.

From *Denver Tribune*, June 6, 1880.

Wyoming Farms, Etc., Etc.

Laramie City, June 10, 1880.

It has snowed a good deal during the week, and it is discouraging to the planters of cotton and tobacco very much. I am positive that a much smaller area of both these staples will be planted in Wyoming this year than ever before. Unless the yield this fall of moss agates and prickly pears should be unusually large, the agricultural export will be very far below preceding years, and there may be actual suffering.

I do not wish to discourage those who might wish to come to this place for the purpose of engaging in agriculture, but frankly I will state that it has its drawbacks.

In the first place, the soil is quite coarse, and the agriculturist, before he can even begin with any prospect of success, must run his farm through a stamp-mill in order to make it sufficiently mellow. This, as the reader will see, involves a large expense at the very outset. Hauling the farm to a custom mill would require a large outlay for teams, and would delay the farmer two or three hundred years in getting his crops in, thus giving the agriculturist who had a pulverized farm in Nebraska, Colorado, or Utah, a great advantage over his own, which had not yet been to the reduction works.

We have, it is true, a large area of farming lands now lying on the dump, but they must first be crushed and then treated for alkali, in which mineral our Wyoming farms are very rich.

Then, again, the climate is erratic, eccentric and peculiar. The altitude is between 7,000 and 8,000 feet above high water mark, so that during the winter it does not snow much, we being above snow line, but in the summer the snow clouds rise above us, and

26

thus the surprised and indignant agriculturist is caught in the middle of a July day with a terrific fall of snow, so that he is virtually compelled to wear his snow shoes all through his haying season.

This is annoying and fatiguing. The snow shoes tread down the grass ahead of him, and make his progress laborious; besides, he tangles his feet up in the winrows, and falls on his nose nine times out of a possible ten.

Again the early frosts make close connections with the late spring blizzards, so that there is only time for a hurried lunch between.

Aside from these little draw backs and the fact that nothing grows without irrigation, except white oak clothes-pins, and promissory notes drawing two per cent interest [per month], the prospect for the agricultural future of Wyoming is indeed gratifying in the extreme . . . .

From *Forty Liars and Other Lies*.

The Parable of the Prodigal Son

Now, there was a certain man who had two sons.

And the younger of them said to his father, "Father, give me the portion of goods that falleth to me."

And he divided unto him his living, and the younger son purchased himself an oil cloth grip-sack and gat him out of that country.

And it came to pass that he journeyed even unto Buckskin and the land that lieth over against Leadville.

And when he was come nigh unto the gates of the city, he heard music and dancing.

And he gat him into that place, and when he arose and went his way, a hireling at the gates smote upon him with a slung-shot of great potency, and the younger son wist not how it was.

Now in the second watch of the night he arose and he was alone, and the pieces of gold and silver were gone.

And it was so.

And he arose and sat down and rent his clothes and threw ashes and dust upon himself.

And he went and joined himself unto a citizen of that country, and he sent him down into a prospect shaft for to dig.

And he had never before dug.

Wherefore, when he spat upon his hands and lay hold of the long-handled shovel wherewith they are wont to shovel, he struck his elbow upon the wall of the shaft wherein he stood, and he poured the earth and the broken rocks over against the back of his neck.

And he waxed exceeding wroth.

And he tried even yet again, and behold! the handle of the shovel became tangled between his legs, and he filled his ear nigh unto full of decomposed slate and porphyry which is in that region round about.

And he wist not why it was so.

Now, after many days the shovelers with their shovels, and the pickers with their picks, and the blasters with their blasts, and the hoisters with their hoists, banded themselves together and each said to his fellow:

Go to! Let us strike. And they stroke.

And they that strake were as the sands of the sea for multitude, and they were terrible as an army with banners.

And they blew upon the ram's horn and the cornet, and sacbut, and the alto horn, and the flute and the brass drum.

Now, it came to pass that the younger son joined not with them which did strike, neither went he out to his work, nor on the highway, lest at any time they that did strike should fall upon him and flatten him out, and send him even unto his home packed in ice, which is after the fashion of that people.

And he began to be in want.

And he went and joined himself unto a citizen of that country; and he sent him into the lunch room to feed tourists.

And he would fain have filled himself up with the adamantine cookies and the indestructible pie and vulcanized sandwiches which the tourists did eat.

And no man gave unto him.

And when he came to himself he said, How many hired servants hath my father on the farm with bread enough and to spare, and I perish with hunger.

And he resigned his position in the lunch business and arose and went unto his father.

But when he was yet a great way off he telegraphed to his father to kill the old cow and make merry, for behold! he had struck it rich, and the old man paid for the telegram.

Now, the elder son was in the north field plowing with a pair of balky mules, and when he came and drew nigh to the house he heard music and dancing.

And he couldn't seem to wot why these things were thus.

And he took the hired girl by the ear and led her away, and asked her, Whence cometh this unseemly hilarity?

And she smote him with the palm of her hand and said: "This thy brother hath come, that was dead and is alive again," and they began to have a high old time.

And the elder son kicked even as the government mule kicketh, and he was hot under the collar, and he gathered up an armful of profanity and flung it in among the guests, and gat him up and girded his loins and lit out.

And he gat him to one learned in the law, and he replevied the entire ranch whereon they were, together with all and singular the hereditaments, right, title, franchise, estate, both in law and in equity, together with all dips, spurs, angles, crooks, variations, leads, veins of gold or silver ore, mill-sites, dam-sites, flumes, and each and every of them firmly by these presents.

And it was so.

From *Bill Nye and Boomerang*.

Catching Mountain Trout at an Elevation of 8000 Feet

A few days ago, in company with Dr. Hayford, I went over to Dale Creek on a brief extempore trouting expedition. Dale Creek is a beautiful and romantic stream running through a rugged canon and crossed by the beautiful iron bridge of the Union Pacific Railroad. We went up on No. 4 and returned on No. 3.

Dale Creek at this season of the year is not very much of a torrent, and on the day we went over there all the trout had gone down to the mouth of the stream to get a drink.

Every little while the Doctor would put on his glasses and hunt for the creek while I caught grasshoppers and looked at the scenery. I did not catch any trout myself, but the Doctor drove one into a prairie-dog hole and killed him. I am frantically fond of field sports although I am not always successful in securing game. I love to wander through the fragrant grass and wild flowers, listening to the song of the bobolink as he sways to and fro on some slender weed; but it delays me a good deal to stop every little while and cut my fly hooks out of my clothes. I throw a fly very gracefully, but when it catches under my shoulder-blades, and I try to lift myself up in that manner, my companions laugh at me and make me mad.

Dr. Hayford, who had command of the expedition, told me that we would have an hour and three quarters to fish and then we would have to go back and catch the train. Therefore we hurried a good deal, and I had to leave a decrepit trout that I had found in a dead pine tree and was almost sure of. We gathered a bouquet of wild roses and ferns and cut worms and went back to the bridge to wait for No. 3. We sat there for an hour or two on a voluptuous triangular fragment of granite, telling large three-ply falsehoods

31

about catching fish and shooting elephants in Michigan. Then we waited two or three more long weary hours, and still the train didn't come.

After a while it occurred to me that I had been made the victim of the man who had spent the most of his life telling the public about the pleasant weather of Wyoming. He enjoyed my misery and cheered me up by saying that perhaps our train had gone, and we would have to wait for the emigrant-train. We ate what lunch we had left, told a few more lies, and suffered on.

At last the thunder of the train in the distance was borne down to us, and we rose with a sigh of relief, gathered up our bouquets and decomposed trout, and prepared to board the car. But it was a work train and didn't stop.

Then I went away by myself and tried to control my fiendish temper. I thought of the doctor's interesting family at home, and how they would mourn if I were to throw him over Dale Creek bridge, and pulverize him on the rocks below. So my better nature conquered and I went back to wait a few more weeks.

The next train that came along was a freight train, and it made better time going past us than at any other point on the road.

Toward evening the regular passenger train came along. I found out which coach the doctor was going to ride in, and I got into another one. I took my poor withered little bouquet and looked at it. All the flowers were dead and so were the bugs that were in it. It was a ghostly ruin that had cost me $9.25. An idea struck me, and I gave the bouquet to the train boy to sell. I told him what the entire array of ghastliness had cost me, and asked him to get what he could out of it.

He took the collection and sold it out to the passengers, realizing $21.35. Passengers bought them and sent them home as flowers collected at Dale Creek bridge in the Rocky mountains. Then a kind hearted gentleman on the train, who saw how sad I looked, and how ragged my clothes were, where I had cut fish-hooks out of them, took up a collection for me.

Hereafter when a man asks me to join a fishing excursion to the mountains, I hope that I shall have the moral courage and strength of character to refuse.

From *Bill Nye and Boomerang.*

The Same Old Thing

Recently I have had the pleasure of acting as chief mourner at a mountain picnic. This subject has been pretty well represented in romance and song already; but I venture to give my experience as being a little out of the ordinary.

The joy which is experienced in the glad, free life of the picknicker is always before the picnic. On the evening before the excursion, he is too full of sacred pleasure and lavender colored tranquillity for anything.

He glides about the house, softly warbling to himself the fragment of some tender love song, while he packs the corkscrews and matches, and other vegetables for the morrow.

I was placed in command of a party of ladies who had everything arranged so that all I needed to do would be to get into the buggy and drive to the mountains, eat my lunch, and drive back again.

I like to go with a party of ladies, because they never make suggestions about the route, or how to drive. They are just as full of gentle trust and child-like confidence and questions as they can be.

They get the lunch ready and get into the buggy, and keep thinking of things they have forgotten, till they get 400 miles from home, and they sing little pieces of old songs, and won't let the great, horrid man in charge of the excursion have any lunch when he gets hungry, because they are hunting for a romantic spot beneath the boughs of a magnificent elm, while every sane man in the Territory knows that there isn't an elm big or little, within $1432\frac{1}{2}$ miles.

We went up in the mountains, because we wanted to go where it would be cool. As a search for a cool resort, this picnic of ours was the most brilliant success. We kept going up at an angle of forty-five degrees from the time we left home until we had to get out and walk to keep warm. We got into one of the upper strata of clouds; and a cold mist mixed with fragments of ice cream, and large chunks of hail and misery, about the size of a burglar-proof safe came gathering over us. Then we camped in the midst of the mountain storm, and the various ladies sat down on their feet, and put the lap robes over them, and looked reproachfully at me. We hovered around the buggy, and two or three little half-grown parasols, and watched the storm. It was a glorious spectacle to the thinking mind.

They began to abuse me because I did not make a circus of myself, and thus drive away the despair and misery of the occasion. They had brought me along, it seemed, because I was such an amusing cuss. It made me a good deal sadder than I would have been otherwise. Here in the midst of a wild and bitter mountain storm, so thick that you couldn't see twenty yards away, with nothing to eat but some marble cake soaked in vinegar, and a piece of cold tongue with a red ant on it, I was expected to make a hippodrome and negro ministrel show of myself. I burst into tears, and tried to sit on my feet as the ladies did. I couldn't do it, so simultaneously and so extemporaneously, as it were, as they could. I had to take them by sections and sit on them. My feet are not large, but at the same time I cannot hover over them both at the same time.

Dear reader, did you ever sit amidst the silence and solitude of the mountains and feel the hailstones rolling down your back, melting and soothing you, and filling your heart with great surging thoughts of the sweet bye-and-bye, and death, and the grave, and other mirth-provoking topics? We had now been about two hundred years without food, it seemed to me, and I mildly suggested that I would like something to eat rather than die of starvation in the midst of plenty; but the ladies wouldn't give me so much as a sam handwich to preserve my life. They told me to smoke if I felt that I must have nourishment, and coldly refused to let me sample the pickled spiders and cold-pressed flies.

So in the midst of all this prepared food I had to go out into the sagebrush and eat raw grasshoppers and greasewood.

Bye and bye, when we concluded that we had seen about all the mountain storm we needed in our business, and didn't pine for any more hail-stones and dampness, we hitched up again and started home. Then we got lost. The ladies felt indignant, but I was delighted. I never was so lost in my life. When I was asked where I thought I was, I could cheerfully reply that I didn't know, and that would stop the conversation for as much as two minutes.

The beauty of being lost is that you are all the time seeing new objects. There is a charm of novelty about being lost that one does not fully understand until he has been there, so to speak.

When I would say that I didn't know where the road led to that we were traveling, one of the party would suggest with mingled bitterness and regret, that we had better turn back. Then I would turn back. I turned back seventeen times at the request of various members of the party for whom I had, and still have, the most unbounded respect.

Finally we got so accustomed to the various objects along this line of travel, that we pined for a change. Then we drove ahead a little farther and found the road. It had been there all the time. It is there yet.

I never had so much fun in all my life. It don't take much to please me, however. I'm of a cheerful disposition, anyhow.

Some of the ladies brought home columbines that had been drowned; others brought home beautiful green mosses with red bugs in them; and others brought home lichens and ferns and neuralgia.

I didn't bring anything home. I was glad to get home myself, and know that I was all there.

I took the lunch basket and examined it. It looked sick and unhappy. At first I thought I would pick the red ants out of the lunch; then I thought it would save time to pick the lunch out of the red ants; but finally I thought I would compromise, by throwing the whole thing into the alley.

I am now preparing a work to be called the "Pick Nicker's Guide; or Starvation Made Easy and Even Desirable!" It will supply a want long felt, and will be within the reach of all.

From *Bill Nye and Boomerang.*

Examining the Brand
of a Frozen Steer

A stock owner went out the other day over the divide to see how his cattle were standing the rigorous weather, and found a large, fine steer in his last long sleep. The stockman had to roll him over to see the brand, and he has regretted his curiosity ever since. He told me that the brand looked to him like a Roman candle making about 2,000 revolutions per moment, and with 187 more prismatic colors than he thought were in existence. Sometimes a steer is not dead but in a cold, sleepy stupor which precedes death, and when stirred up a little and irritated because he cannot die without turning over and showing his brand, he musters his remaining strength and kicks the inquisitive stockman so high he can see and recognize the features of departed friends. That was the way it happened on this occasion. The stockman fell in the branches of a pine tree on Jack Creek, not dead but very thoughtful. He said he was near enough to hear the rush of wings, and was just going to register and engage a room in the New Jerusalem when he returned to consciousness.

From *Bill Nye and Boomerang*.

Fine-Cut as a Means of Grace

The amateur tobacco chewer many times through lack of consideration allows himself to be forced into very awkward and unpleasant positions. As a fair sample of the perils to which the young and inexperienced masticator of the weed is subjected, the following may be given:

A few Sabbaths ago a young man who was attending divine worship up on Piety Avenue, concluded, as the sermon was about one-half done and didn't seem to get very exciting, that he would take a chew of tobacco. He wasn't a handsome chewer, and while he was sliding the weed out of his pocket and getting it behind his handkerchief and working it into his mouth, he looked as though he might be robbing a blind woman of her last copper. Then when he got it into his mouth and tried to look pious and anxious about the welfare of his never dying soul, the chew in his mouth felt as big as a Magnolia ham. Being new in the business, the salivary glands were so surprised that they began to secrete at a remarkable rate. The young man got alarmed. He wanted to spit. His eyes began to hang out on his cheek, and still the salivary glands continued to give down. He thought about spitting in his handkerchief or his hat, but neither seemed to answer the purpose. He was getting wild. He thought of swallowing it, but he knew that his stomach wasn't large enough.

In his madness he resolved that he would let drive down the aisle when the pastor looked the other way. He waited till the divine threw his eyes toward heaven and then he shut his eyes and turned loose. An old gentleman about three pews down the aisle yawned at that moment and threw his open hand out into the aisle in such a manner as to catch the contribution without any loss to speak of. He did not put his hand out for that purpose and did not seem to want it, but he got it all right.

He seemed to feel hurt about something. He looked like a man who had suddenly lost faith in humanity and become soured, as it were. Some who sat near him said he swore. Anyway, he lost the thread of the discourse. That part of the sermon he now says is a blank to him. It is several blanks. He called upon blank to ever-lastingly blank such a blankety blank blank, idiotic blank fool as the young man was.

Meantime the young man quit the use of tobacco. He did not know at first whether to swear off or kill himself. The other day he said: "Only two weeks ago I stood up and said proudly I ama-teur. Today, praise be to redeeming grace, I am not a chewer." (This joke for the first few days will have to be watered very care-fully and wrapped in a California blanket, for it is not strong at all. However, if it can be worked through the cold weather it is no slouch of a joke.)

From *Bill Nye and Boomerang.*

My Mine

I located a claim called the Boomerang. I named it after my favorite mule. I call my mule Boomerang because he has such an eccentric orbit and no one can tell just when he will clash with some other heavenly body.

He has a sigh like the long drawn breath of a fog-horn. He likes to come to my tent in the morning about daylight and sigh in my ear before I am awake. He is a highly amusing little cuss, and it tickles him a good deal to pour about $13\frac{1}{2}$ gallons of his melody into my ear while I am dreaming, sweetly dreaming. He enjoys my look of pleasant surprise when I wake up.

He would cheerfully pour more than $13\frac{1}{2}$ gallons of sigh into my ear, but that is all my ear will hold. There is nothing small about Boomerang. He is generous to a fault and lavishes his low, sad, tremulous wail on every one who has time to listen to it.

Those who have never been wakened from a sweet, sweet dream by the low sad wail of a narrow-gauge mule, so close to the ear that the warm breath of the songster can be felt on the cheek, do not know what it is to be loved by a patient, faithful, dumb animal.

The first time he rendered this voluntary for my benefit, I rose in my wrath and some other clothes, and went out and shot him. I discharged every chamber of my revolver into his carcass, and went back to bed to wait till it got lighter. In a couple of hours I arose and went out to bury Boomerang. The remains were off about twenty yards eating bunch grass. In the gloom and uncertainty of night, I had shot six shots into an old windlass near a deserted shaft.

Boomerang and I get along first-rate together. When I am lonesome I shoot at him, and when he is lonesome he comes up and lays his head across my shoulder, and looks at me with great soulful eyes and sings to me.

From *Bill Nye and Boomerang*.

The Nocturnal Cow

With the opening up of my spring movements in the agricultural line comes the cow.

Laramie has about seven cows that annoy me a good deal. They work me up so that I lose my equanimity. I have mentioned this matter before, but this spring the trouble seems to have assumed some new features. The prevailing cow for this season seems to be a seal-brown cow with a stub tail, which is arranged as a night-key. She wears it banged.

The other day I had just planted my celluloid radishes and irrigated my novel bengal turnips and sown my hunting-case summer squashes, and this cow went by trying to convey the impression that she was out for a walk.

That night the blow fell. The queen of night was high in the blue vault of heaven amid the twinkling stars. All nature was hushed to repose. The people of Laramie were in their beds. So were my hunting-case summer squashes. I heard a stealthy step near the conservatory where my celluloid radishes and pickled beets are growing, and I arose.

*   *   *   *   *

It was a lovely sight. At the head of the procession there was a seal-brown cow with a tail like the handle on a pump, and standing at an angle of forty-five degrees.

That was the cow.

Following at a rapid gait was a bewitching picture of alabaster limbs and Gothic joints and Wamsutta muslin night robe.

That was me.

The queen of night withdrew behind a cloud.

The vision seemed to break her all up.

41

Bye-and-bye there was a crash, and the seal-brown cow went home carrying the garden gate with her as a kind of keepsake. She had a plenty of garden gates at home in her collection, but she had none of that particular pattern. So she wore it home around her neck.

The writer of these lines then carefully brushed the sand off his feet with a pillow sham and retired to rest.

When the bright May morn was ushered in upon the busy world the radish and squash bed had melted into chaos and there only remained some sticks of stove wood and the tracks of a cow, interspersed with the dainty little foot prints of some Peri or other who evidently stepped about four yards at a lick, and could wear a number nine shoe if necessary.

Yesterday morning it was very cold, and when I went out to feed my royal self-acting hen, I found this same cow wedged into the hen coop. O, blessed opportunity! O, thrice blessed and long-sought revenge!

Now I had her where she could not back out, and I secured a large picket from the fence, and took my coat off, and breathed in a full breath. I did not want to kill her, I simply wanted to make her wish that she had died of membranous croup when she was young.

While I was spitting on my hands she seemed to catch my idea, but she saw how hopeless was her position. I brought down the picket with the condensed strength and eagerness and wrath of two long, suffering years. It struck the corner of the hen-house. There was a deafening crash and then all was still, save the low, rippling laugh of the cow, as she stood in the alley and encouraged me while I nailed up the hen-house again.

Looking back over my whole life, it seems to me that it is strewn with nothing but the rugged ruins of my busted anticipations.

From *Bill Nye and Boomerang*.

Apostrophe to An Orphan Mule

Oh! lonely, gentle, unobtrusive mule!
Thou standest idly 'gainst the azure sky,
And sweetly, sadly singeth like a hired man.
    Who taught thee thus to warble
In the noontide heat and wrestle with
Thy deep, corroding grief and joyless woe?
Who taught thy simple heart
    Its pent-up, wildly-warring waste
Of wanton woe to carol forth upon
        The silent air?
    I chide thee not, because the
Song is fraught with grief-embittered
Monotone and joyless minor chords
Of wild, imported melody, for thou
Art restless, woe begirt and
Compassed round about with gloom,
    Thou timid, trusting, orphan mule!
        Few joys indeed, are thine,
Thou thrice-bestricken, madly-
Mournful, melancholy mule.
And he alone who strews
Thy pathway with his cold remains
Can give thee recompense
    Of melancholy woe.
He who hath sought to steer
Thy limber, yielding tail
Ferninst thy crupper-band
    Hath given thee joy, and he alone.
'Tis true, he may have shot
Athwart the Zodiac, and, looking
O'er the outer walls upon

The New Jerusalem,
Have uttered vain regrets.
Thou reckest not, O orphan mule,
For it hath given thee joy, and
Bound about thy bursting heart,
And held thy tottering reason
        To its throne.
Sing on, O mule, and warble
In the twilight gray,
Unchidden by the heartless throng.
Sing of thy parents on thy father's side,
Yearn for the days now past and gone;
For he who pens these halting,
Limping lines to thee
Doth bid thee yearn, and yearn, and yearn.

From *Bill Nye and Boomerang*.

Hong Lee's Grand Benefit at Leadville

It will be remembered that about nine months ago Hong Lee resolved to establish a branch laundry and shirt-destroying establishment in Leadville, with the main office and general headquarters in Laramie. All at once he came back, and seemed to be satisfied at the old stand. So I would ask him his opinion of the future of the carbonate camps.

Hong Lee had just tied his hair up in a Grecian coil and secured it in a mass of shining braids, as I came in, and was giving some orders as to the day's work. One employe was just completing his devotions to a cross-eyed god in one corner, and another was squirting water out of his mouth like an oriental street sprinkler over the spotless front of a white shirt.

Hong Lee asked me to sit down on the ironing table and make myself at home. I asked him how trade was, and a few other unimportant questions, and then asked him what he thought of Leadville. I cannot give the conversation in the exact language in which it was given, as I am not up in pigeon English. He said he went over to Leadville, thinking that at $4.25 per dozen he could work up a good business and wear a brocaded overshirt with slashed sleeves and Pekin trimmings. Trade was a little dull here and he had more Chinamen than he could use, so he had concluded to establish a branch outfit at Leadville and make some scads.

I asked him why he did not remain at the camp and go through the programme.

He said that the general feeling in Leadville was not friendly to the Chinaman. The people did not meet him with a brass band, and the mayor didn't tender him the freedom of the city. On the contrary, they seemed cold and distant toward him. By and by they clubbed together and came to call on him. They were very attentive then. Very much so. Some had shot-guns to fire salutes with, and others had large clotheslines in their hands. Hong Lee felt proud to be so much thought of, and was preparing an impromptu speech on orange paper with a marking brush, when the chairman came and told him that a few American citizens had come, hoping to be of use to him in learning the ways of the city.

Then they took him out to the public square where Hong Lee supposed that he was to make his speech, and they proceeded to kick him into the most shapeless mass. They kicked him into a globular form, and then flattened him out, after which they knocked him into a rhomboid. This change was followed by thumping him into an isosceles triangle. When he looked more like a bundle of old clothes than a Chinaman, they took him with a pair of tongs, and threw him over the battlements.

Hong Lee returned to consciousness, and murmured, "Where am I?" or words to that effect. A noble mule-skinner passing by, touched him up with the hot end of his mule whip, and showed him the route to Denver.

Hong Lee says now, be it ever so humble, there's no place like home.

From *Bill Nye and Boomerang.*

The Rocky Mountain Hog

In speaking of the domestic and useful animals of Laramie, it would not be right to overlook the hog. I do not allude to him as useful at all, but he is very domestic. He is more so than the people seem to demand. I never saw hogs with such a strong domestic tendency as the Laramie hogs have. They have a deep and abiding love for home, all of them, and they don't care whose home it is either.

There is a tremendous pressure of hog to the square inch here. The town is filled with homeless, unhappy and starving hogs. They run between your legs during the day, and stand in your front yard and squeal during the night. Most of them are orphans When Thanksgiving comes it will bring no joy to them. It will be like any other day. About all the fun they have is to root a gate off the hinges, and then run off with a table cloth in their mouths. We should not be too severe, however, on the hog. What means has he of knowing that there is a city ordinance against his running about town? Kind reader, do you think the innocent little hog would openly violate a law of the land if he knew of its existence? Certainly not. It is pardonable ignorance on the part of the hog, the same as it is with the Indian, which causes him to break over the statutes and ordinances of his country.

Our plan, therefore is to CIVILIZE THE HOG. Build churches and school houses for him. Educate him and teach him the ways of industry. Put a spade and plow at his disposal, and teach him to till the soil. The natural impulses of the hog are good, but he has been imposed upon by dishonest white men.

Did you ever stop to think, dear reader, that the hog of the present day is but a poor, degraded specimen of the true aboriginal hog, before civilization had encroached upon him? Then do not join the popular cry against him. Once he was pure as the beautiful snow.

From *Bill Nye and Boomerang*.

The Temperature of the Bumble-Bee

A recent article on bees says, "If you have noticed bees very closely, you may have seen that they are not all alike in size."

I have noticed bees very closely indeed, during my life. In fact I have several times been thrown into immediate juxtaposition with them, and have had a great many opportunities to observe their ways, and I am free to say that I have not been so forcibly struck with the difference in their size as the noticeable difference in their temperature.

I remember at one time of sitting by a hive watching the habits of the bees, and thinking how industrious they were, and what a wide difference there is between the toilsome life of the little insect, and the enervating, aimless, idle and luxurious life of the newspaper man, when an impulsive little bee lit in my hair. He seemed to be feverish. Wherever he settled down he seemed to leave a hot place. I learned afterward that it was a new kind of bee called the anti-clinker base-burner bee.

O, yes, I have studied the ways of the bee very closely. He is supposed to improve each shining hour. That's the great objection I have to him. The bee has been thrown up to me a great deal during my life, and the comparison was not flattering. It has been intimated that I resembled the bee that sits on the piazza of the hive all summer and picks his teeth, while the rest are getting in honey and bees-wax for the winter campaign.

From *Bill Nye and Boomerang*.

Suggestions for a School
of Journalism

A number of friends having personally asked me to express an opinion upon the matter of an established school of journalism, as spoken of by ex-Mayor Henry C. Robinson, of Hartford, Connecticut, and many more through the West who are strangers to me personally, having written me to give my views upon the subject, I have consented in so far that I will undertake a simple synopsis of what the course should embrace.

I most heartily indorse the movement, if it may be called such at this early stage. Knowing a little of the intricacies of this branch of the profession, I am going to state fully my belief as to its importance, and the necessity for a thorough training upon it. We meet almost everywhere newspaper men who are totally unfitted for the high office of public educators through the all-powerful press. The woods is full of them. We know that not one out of a thousand of those who are to-day classed as journalists is fit for that position.

I know that to be the case, because people tell me so.

I cannot call to mind to-day, in all my wide journalistic acquaintance, a solitary man who has not been pronounced an ass by one or more of my fellow-men. This is indeed a terrible state of affairs.

In many instances these harsh criticisms are made by those who do not know, without submitting themselves to a tremendous mental strain, the difference between a "lower case" q and the old Calvinistic doctrine of unanimous damnation, but that makes no difference; the true journalist should strive to please the masses. He should make his whole life a study of human nature and an earnest effort to serve the great reading world collectively and individually.

This requires a man, of course, with similar characteristics and the same general information possessed by the Almighty, but who would be willing to work at a much more moderate salary.

The reader will instantly see how difficult it is to obtain this class of men. Outside of the mental giant who writes these lines and two or three others, perhaps——

But never mind. I leave a grateful world to say that, while I map out a plan for the ambitious young journalist who might be entering upon the broad arena of newspaperdom, and preparing himself at a regularly established school for that purpose.

Let the first two years be devoted to meditation and prayer. This will prepare the young editor for the surprise and consequent profanity which in a few years he may experience when he finds in his boss editorial that God is spelled with a little g, and the peroration of the article has been taken out and carefully locked up between a death notice and the announcement of the birth of a cross-eyed infant.

The ensuing five years should be spent in becoming familiar with the surprising and mirth-provoking orthography of the English language.

Then would follow three years devoted to practice with dumb bells, sand bags and slung shots, in order to become an athlete. I have found in my own journalistic history more cause for regret over my neglect of this branch than any other. I am a pretty good runner, but aside from that I regret to say that as an athlete I am not a dazzling success.

The above course of intermediate training would fit the student to enter upon the regular curriculum.

Then set aside ten years for learning the typographical art perfectly, so that when visitors wish to look at the composing room, and ask the editor to explain the use of the "hell box," he will not have to blush and tell a gauzy lie about its being a composing stick. Let the young journalist study the mysteries of type setting, distributing, press work, galleys, italic, shooting sticks, type lice and other mechanical implements of the printer's department.

Five years should be spent in learning to properly read and correct proof, as well as how to mark it on the margin like a Chinese map of the Gunnison country.

At least fifteen years should then be devoted to the study of American politics and the whole civil service. This time could be extended five years with great profit to the careful student who wishes, of course, to know thoroughly the names and records of all public men, together with the relative political strength of each party.

He should then take a medical course and learn how to bind up contusions, apply arnica, court plaster or bandages, plug up bullet holes and prospect through the human system for buck shot. The reason of this course which should embrace five years of close study, is apparent to the thinking mind.

Ten years should then be devoted to the study of law. No thorough metropolitan editor wants to enter upon his profession without knowing the difference between a writ of *mandamus* and other styles of profanity. He should thoroughly understand the entire system of American jurisprudence, and be as familiar with the more recent decisions of the courts as New York people are with the semi-annual letter of Governor Seymour declining the Presidency.

The student will by this time begin to see what is required of him and will enter with greater zeal upon his adopted profession.

He will now enter upon a theological course of ten years. He can then write a telling editorial on the great question of What We Shall Do To Be Saved without mixing up Calvin and Tom Paine with Judas Iscariot and Ben Butler.

The closing ten years of the regular course might be profitably used in learning a practical knowledge of cutting cord wood, baking beans, making shirts, lecturing, turning double handsprings, preaching the gospel, learning how to make a good adhesive paste that will not sour in hot weather, learning the art of scissors grinding, punctuation, capitalization, prosody, plain sewing, music, dancing, sculping, etiquette, how to win the affections of the opposite sex, the ten commandments, every man his own teacher on the violin, croquet, rules of the prize ring, parlor magic, civil engineering, decorative art, calsomining, bicycling, base ball, hydraulics, botany, poker, calisthenics, high-low jack, international law, faro, rhetoric, fifteen-ball pool, drawing and painting, mule skinning, vocal music, horsemanship, plastering, bull whacking, etc., etc., etc.

At the age of 95 the student will have lost that wild, reckless and impulsive style so common among younger and less experienced journalists. He will emerge from the school with a light heart and a knowledge-box loaded up to the muzzle with the most useful information.

The hey day and springtime of life will, of course, be past, but the graduate will have nothing to worry him any more, except the horrible question which is ever rising up before the journalist, as to whether he shall put his money into government four per cents or purchase real estate in some growing town.

From *Bill Nye and Boomerang*.

The Buckness Wherewith
the Buck Beer Bucketh

Buck beer is demoralizing in its tendency when it moveth itself aright. It layeth hold of the intellect and twisteth it out of shape.

My son, go not with them who go to seek buck beer, for at the last it stingeth like the brocaded hornet with the red-hot narrative, and kicketh like the choleric mule.

Who hath woe? Who hath babbling? Who hath redness of eyes? He that goeth to seek the schooner of buck beer.

Who hath sorrow? Who striveth when the middle watch of the night hath come, to wind up the clock with the 15 puzzle?

He that kicketh against the buck beer and getteth left.

Verily, the buckness of the buck beer bucketh with a mighty buck, insomuch that the buckee riseth at the noon hour with a head that compasseth the town round about, and the swellness thereof waxeth more and more, even from Dan to Beer—sheba. (Current joke in the Holy Land.)

Who clamoreth with a loud voice and saith, verily, am not I a bad man? Who is he that walketh unsteadily and singeth unto himself, "The bright angels are waiting for me"? Who wotteth not even a fractional wot, but setteth his chronometer with the wooden watch of the watchmaker, and by means of a toothbrush?

Go to. Is it not he who bangeth his intellect ferninst the bock beer, even unto the eleventh hour?

From *Bill Nye and Boomerang.*

The Lop-Eared Lovers
of the Little Laramie

A TALE OF LOVE AND PARENTAL CUSSEDNESS

CHAPTER I

The scene opens with a landscape. In the foreground stands a house; but there are no honeysuckles or Johnny-jump-ups clambering over the door; there are no Columbines or bitter-sweets, or bachelors-buttons, clinging lovingly to the eaves, and filling the air with fragrance. The reason for this is, that it is too early in the spring for Columbines and Johnny-jump-ups, at the time when our story opens, and they wouldn't grow in that locality without irrigation, anyway. That is the reason that these little adjuncts do not appear in the landscape.

But the scene is nevertheless worthy of a painter. The house, especially, ought to be painted, and a light coat of the same article on the front gate would improve its appearance materially. In the door of the cottage stands a damsel, whose natural loveliness is enhanced 30 or 40 per cent. by a large oroide chain which encircles her swan-like throat; and, as she shades her eyes with her alabaster hand, the gleam of a gutta percha ring on her front finger tells the casual observer that *she is engaged.*

While she is shading her eyes from the blinding glare of the orb of day, the aforesaid orb of day keeps right on setting, according to advertisement, and at last disappears behind the snowy range, lighting up, as it does so, the fleecy clouds and turning them into gold, figuratively speaking, making the picture one of surpassing loveliness. But what does she care for a $13.00 sunset, or the low,

55

sad wail of the sage-hen far up the canon, as it calls for its mate? What does she care for the purple landscape and the mournful sigh of the new milch cow which is borne to her over the green divide? She don't care a cent.

CHAPTER II

It is now the proper time to bring in the solitary horseman. He is seen riding a mouse-colored bronco on a smooth canter, and, from his uneasiness in the saddle, it is evident that he has been riding a long time, and that it doesn't agree with him. He has been attending the spring meeting of the Rocky Mountain Roundup.

He takes a benevolent chew of tobacco, looks at his cylinder-escapement watch, and plunges his huge Mexican spurs into the panting sides of his bronco steed. The ambitious steed rears forward and starts away into the gathering gloom at the rate of twenty-one miles in twenty-one days, while a bitter oath escapes from the clenched teeth and foam-flecked lips of the pigeon-toed rider.

But stay! Let us catch a rapid outline of the solitary horseman, for he is the affianced lover and soft-eyed gazelle of Luella Frowzletop, the queen of the Skimmilk Ranche. He is evidently a man of say twenty summers, with a sinister expression to the large, ambitious, imported Italian mouth. A broad-brimmed white hat with a scarlet flannel band protects his Gothic features from the burning sun, and a pale-brown ducking suit envelopes his lithe form. A horsehair lariat hangs at his saddle bow, and the faint suspicion of a downy mustache on his chiselled upper lip is just beginning to ooze out into the air, as if ashamed of itself. It is one of those sickly mustaches, a kind of cross between blonde and brindle, which mean well enough, but never amount to anything. His eyes are fierce and restless, with short, expressive, white eye-lashes, and his nose is short but wide out, gradually melting away into his bronzed and stalwart cheeks, like a dish of ice-cream before a Sabbath school picnic.

Such is the rough sketch of Pigeon-toed Pete, the swain who had stolen away the heart of Luella Frowzletop, the queen of Skim-milk Ranche. He isn't handsome, but he is very good, and he loves the fair Luella with a great deal of diligence, although her parents are averse to the match, for we might as well inform the sagacious and handsome reader that her parents are Presbyterians, whereas the hero of this blood-curdling tale is a hard-shell Baptist. Thus are two hearts doomed to love in vain.

CHAPTER III

During all this time that we have been going on with the preceding chapter, Luella has been standing in the door looking away to the eastward, a soiled gingham apron thrown over her head, and a dreamy, far-away look in her mournful sorrel eyes. Suddenly there breaks on her finely moulded and flexible ear the sound of a horse's hoof.

"Aha!" she murmurs. "Hist! it is him. Blast his picture! Why didn't he have some style about him, and get here on time?" And she impatiently mashes a huge mosquito that is fastened on her swarthy arm.

Any one could see, as she stood there, that she was mad. She didn't really have any cause for it, but she was an only child, and accustomed to being petted and humored, and lying in bed till half past ten. This had made her high spirited, and she occasionally turned loose with the first thing that came to hand.

"You're a fine haired snoozer from Bitter Creek; ain't ye?" said the pale flower of Skimmilk Ranche, as the solitary horseman alighted from his panting steed, and threw his arms about her with great *sang froid*.

"In what respect?" said Pigeon-toed Pete, as he held her from him, and looked lovingly down into her deep, sorrel eyes.

"O fairest of thy sect," he continued, as he took out his quid of tobacco, preparatory to planting a long, wide, passionate kiss on her burning cheek, "you wot not what you fain would say. The way was long, my ambling steed has a ringbone on the off leg, and thou chidest me, thy erring swain, without a cause." He knew that she would pitch into him, so he had this little impromptu speech all committed to memory.

She pillowed her sunny head on his panting breast for an hour or so, and shed eleven or eight happy tears.

"O lode star of my existence, and soother of my every sorrow," said he, with charming *naïveté*, "wilt thou fly with me to-night to some adjacent justice of the peace, and be my skipful gazelle, my little *ne plus ultra*, my own *magnum bonum* and *multum in parvo*, so to speak? Leave your Presbyterian parents to run the ranche, and fly with me. You shall never want for anything. You shall never put your dimpled hands in dish-water, or wring out your own clothes. I will get you a new rosewood washing machine, and when your slightest look indicates that you want forty or fifty dollars for pin money, I will make out a check for that amount."

He had just finished his little harangue, whatever that is, and was putting in a few choice gestures, when the old man came around from behind the rain-water barrel with a shot-gun, and told the ardent admirer of Luella that he had better not linger to any great extent, and as he said it in his quiet but firm way, at the same time fondling the lock on his shot-gun, the lover lingered not, but hied him away to his neighing steed, and lightly springing into the saddle, was soon lost to the sight. We will leave him on the road for a short time.

*   *   *   *   *

CHAPTER IV

We will now suppose a period of three years to have passed. Luella had been sent to visit her friends in southern Iowa, partly to assuage her grief, and partly to save expenses, for she was a hearty eater. Here she met a young man named Rufus G. Hopper, who fell in love with her, about the first hard work he did, and when, metaphorically speaking, he laid his 40-acre homestead, with its wealth of grasshopper eggs, at her feet, she capitulated, and became his'n, and he became her'n.

Thus these two erstwhile lovers of the long ago had become separated, and the fair Queen of the Skimmilk Ranche had taken a change of venue with her affections. Still all seemed to be well to the casual observer, although at times her eyes had that far-away look of those who are crossed in love, or whose livers are out of order. Was it the fleeing vision of the absent lover, or had she eaten something that didn't agree with her?

Ah! who shall say that at times there did not flash across her mind the fact that she had sacrificed herself on the altar of Mammon, and given her rich love in exchange for forty acres of Government land? But the time drew nigh for the celebration of the nuptials, and still no tidings of the absent lover. Nearer and nearer came the 4th of July, the day set apart for the wedding, and still in the dark mysterious bosom of the unknown, lurked the absent swain.

*   *   *   *   *

These stars indicate the number of days which we must now suppose to have passed, and the glad day of the Nation's rejoicing is at hand. The loud mouthed cannon proclaims, for the one hundredth time, that in the little Revolutionary scrimmage of 1776, our forefathers got away with the persimmons. Flags wave, bands play, and crackers explode, and scare the teams from the country. Fair rustic maids are seen on every hand with their good clothes on, and farmers' sons walk up and down the street, asking the price of watermelons and soda water. Bye and bye the band comes down street playing "Old Zip Coon," with variations. The procession begins to form and point toward the grand stand, where the Declaration of Independence will be read to the admiring audience, and lemonade retailed at five cents a glass.

But who are the couple who sit on the front seat near the speaker's stand, listening with rapt attention to the new and blood-curdling romance, entitled the "Declaration of Independence?" It is Luella and her new husband. The casual observer can discover that, by the way he smokes a cheap cigar in her face, and allows the fragrant smoke from the five cent Havana to drift into her sorrel eyes. All at once the band strikes up the operatic strain of "Captain Jinks," and as the sad melody dies away in the distance, a young man steps proudly forth, at the conclusion of the president's introductory speech, and in a low, musical voice, begins to set forth the wrongs visited on the Pilgrim Fathers, and to dish up the bones of G. Washington and T. Jefferson, in various styles.

What is it about the classic mouth, with its charming *naïveté* and the amber tinge lurking about its roguish outlines, which awakes the old thrill in Luella's heart, and causes the vital current to recede from its accustomed channels, and leave her face like marble, save where here and there a large freckle stands out in bold relief? It is the mouth of Pigeon-toed Pete. Those same Gothic features stand out before her, and she knows him in a moment. It is true he had colored his mustache, and he wore a stand-up collar; but it was the same form, the same low, musical, squeaky voice, and the same large, intellectual ears, which she remembered so well.

It appeared that he had been to the Gunnison country, and having manifested considerable originality and genius as a bull whacker, had secured steady employment and large wages, being a man with a ready command of choice and elegant profanity, and an irresistible way of appealing to the wants of a sluggish animal. Taking his spare change, he had invested it in hand made sour mash corn juice, which he retailed at from 25 to 50 cents a glass. Rain water being plenty, the margin was large, and his profits highly satisfactory. In this way he had managed to get together some cash, and was at once looked upon as a leading capitalist, and a man on whom rested the future prosperity of the country. He wore moss-agate sleeve buttons, and carried a stem-winding watch. He looked indeed like a thing of life, and as he closed with some stirring quotation from Martin F. Tupper amid the crash of applause, and the band struck up the oratorio of "Whoop 'em up 'Liza Jane," the audience dispersed to witness a game of base-ball. Luella took her husband's arm, climbed into the lumber wagon, and rode home, with a great grief in her heart. Had she deferred her wedding for only a few short hours, the course of her whole life would have been entirely changed, and, instead of plodding her weary way through the long, tedious years as Mrs. Hopper, making rag-carpets during winter, and smashing the voracious potato bug during the summer, she might have been interested in a carbonate Bonanza, worn checked stockings, and low-necked shoes.

There are two large, limpid tears standing in her sorrel eyes, as the curtain falls on this story, and her lips move involuntarily as she murmurs that little couplet from Milton:

> "I feel kind of sad and bilious, because
> My heart keeps sighing, 'It couldn't was.'"

From *Bill Nye and Boomerang*.

Queer

An exchange says that the people of that locality were considerably excited the other day over a three-cornered dog fight that occurred there. This is not surprising. Had it been simply a combat between oblong or rectangular dogs, or even a short but common-place fight between rhombohedral or octagonal dogs it would not have attracted any attention, but an engagement between triangular dogs is something that calls forth our wonder and surprise.

From *Bill Nye and Boomerang*.

The Weather and Some Other Things

Sometimes I wish that Wyoming had more vegetation and less catarrh, more bloom and summer and fragrance and less Christmas and New Year's through the summer.

I like the clear, bracing air of 7,500 feet [Laramie's altitude is 7,165 feet] above the civilized world, but I get weary of putting on and taking off my buffalo overcoat for meals all through dog days. I yearn for a land where a man can take off his ulster and overshoes while he delivers a Fourth of July oration, without flying into the face of Providence and dying of pneumonia.

Perhaps I am unreasonable, but I can't help it. I have my own peculiar notions, and I am not to blame for them.

As I write these lines I look out across the wide sweep of brownish gray plains dotted here and there with ranches and defunct buffalo craniums, and I see shutting down over the sides of the abrupt mountains, and meeting the foothills, a white mist which melts into the gray sky. It is a snow storm in the mountains.

I saw this with wonder and admiration for the first two or three million times. When it became a matter of daily occurrence as a wonder or curiosity, it was below mediocrity. Last July a snow storm gathered one afternoon and fell among the foothills and whitened the whole line to within four or five miles of town, and it certainly was a peculiar freak of nature, but it convinced me that whatever enterprises I might launch into here I would not try to raise oranges and figs until the isothermal lines should meet with a change of heart . . . .

From *Bill Nye and Boomerang*.

Some Thoughts on Childhood

Childhood is the glad springtime of life. It is then that the seeds of future greatness or startling mediocrity are sown.

If a boy has marked out a glowing future as an intellectual giant, it is during these early years of his growth that he gets some pine knots to burn in the evening, whereby he can read Herbert Spencer and the Greek grammar, so that when he is in good society he can say things that nobody can understand. This gives him an air of mysterious greatness which soaks into those with whom he comes in contact, and makes them respectful and unhappy while in his presence.

Boys who intend to be railroad men should early begin to look about them for some desirable method of expunging two or three fingers and one thumb. Most boys can do this without difficulty. Trying to pick a card out of a job press when it is in operation is a good way. Most job presses feel gloomy and unhappy until they have eaten the fingers off two or three boys. Then they go on with their work cheerfully and even hilariously.

Boys who intend to lead an irreproachable life and be foremost in every good word and work, should take unusual precautions to secure perfect health and longevity. Good boys never know when they are safe. Statistics show that the ratio of good boys who die, compared to bad ones, is simply appalling.

There are only thirty-nine good boys left as we go to press, and they are not feeling very well either.

The bad ones are all alive and very active.

The boy who stole my coal shovel last spring and went out into the grave-yard and dug into a grave to find Easter eggs, is the picture of health. He ought to live a long time yet, for he is in very poor shape to be ushered in before the bar of judgment.

When I was a child I was different from other boys in many respects. I was always looking about to see what good I could do. I am that way yet.

If my little brother wanted to go in swimming contrary to orders, I was not strong enough to prevent him, but I would go in with him and save him from a watery grave. I went in the water thousands of times that way, and as a result he is alive to-day.

But he is ungrateful. He hardly ever mentions it now, but he remembers the gordian knots that I tied in his shirts. He speaks of them frequently. This shows the ingratitude and natural depravity of the human heart.

Ah, what recompense have wealth and position for the unalloyed joys of childhood, and how gladly to-day as I sit in the midst of my oriental splendor and costly magnificence, and thoughtfully run my fingers through my infrequent bangs, would I give it all, wealth, position and fame, for one balmy, breezy day gathered from the mellow haze of the long ago when I stood full knee-deep in the luke-warm pool near my suburban home in the quiet dell, and allowed the yielding and soothing mud and meek-eyed pollywogs to squirt up between my dimpled toes.

From *Bill Nye and Boomerang*.

A Christmas Ride in July

I've just returned from a long ride to the Soda Lakes.

The ride reminded me of a tour I took in July from Laramie over to Cheyenne, two years ago. We had experienced the pleasure of riding over the mountain, on the Union Pacific train, and had held our breath while crossing Dale Creek bridge, and viewed with wonder the broken billows of granite, lying here and there at the tip-top of the mighty divide. But some one had said that it was nothing compared with the mirth-provoking trip by carriage across the mountains, over a fine wagon road to Cheyenne.

In the morning I nearly melted riding up the sandy canyon, and took off my coat and gliding pleasantly along, alternately sang one or two low throbs of melody, and alternately swore about the extreme heat.

When we got nearly to the top, I thought it didn't look well for a man to whom the American people look for so much in the future, to be riding along the public highway without his coat, so I put it on. At the top of the mountain I put on a linen duster and gloves. Shortly after that I put on my overshoes and a sealskin cap. Later, I put on my buffalo overcoat, and got out and ran behind the carriage to keep warm.

When I got to Cheyenne, the Doctor looked me over and said that he could save my feet because they had so much vitality, and were in such a good state of preservation; but my ears—my pride and glory—the ears that I had defended through the newspapers for years, and had stood up for when all about was dark—they had to go.

That is, part of them had to go, and there was enough left to hear with; but the ornamental scallops and box plaiting, and frills, the wainscoting, and royal Corinthian entablatures had to go.

From *Bill Nye and Boomerang.*

The Gentle Youth from Leadville

In addition to the other attractions about the depot, the old museum of curiosities from the Rocky Mountains has been re-opened. I like to go down and listen to the remarks of the overland passenger relative to these articles. There are two stuffed coyotes chained to the door, one on each side, and it amuses me to see a solicitous parent nearly yank his little son to pieces for going so near these ferocious animals. The coyotes look very life-like, and show their teeth a good deal, but it breaks a man all up when he finds that their digestive apparatus has been replaced with sawdust and plaster of Paris.

After a coyote gets to padding himself out with baled hay and cotton so as to look plump, he loses his elasticity of spirits, and we cease to respect him. Sometimes a tourist asks if these coyotes are prairie dogs.

A few days ago a man from Michigan, who has been here two weeks and wears a large buckskin patch where it will do the most good, and who is very bitter in his remarks about "tenderfeet," was standing at the depot, when a young man, evidently from a theological seminary, came along from the train whistling, "What a friend we have in Jesus." He walked up to the Michigan man, who began to look fierce, and timidly asked if he would tell him all about the coyote. The Michigan man, who never had seen a live coyote in his life, volunteered to tell him some of the finest decorated lies, with venetian blinds and other trimmings to them, while the young man stood there in open-mouthed wonder, with daylight visible between his legs as high as the fifth rib. I never saw such a picture of rapt attention in my life. As he became more interested, the Michigan man warmed up to his work and lied to this guileless youth till the perspiration rolled down his face. As

66

the train started out, the delegate to the Young Men's Christian Association asked the Michigan man for his address. "I want the address of some good earnest liar," he said, "one who can lie by the day, or by the job, and endure the strain. I want a man to enter the field for the championship of America. Any communication you may wish to make will reach me at Leadville, Colorado. I have been in the Rocky Mountains ever since I was three years old, and have lived for weeks with no other diet but coyote on toast and raw Michigan man." He waved his hand at the M. man, and said: "If I don't see you again, hello!" and he was gone.

How many such little episodes we experience on our journey to the tomb.

From *Bill Nye and Boomerang.*

Home-Made Indian Relics

Sherman, on the Union Pacific Railroad, is the loftiest by a considerable majority of any point on the road. This fact has occasioned some little notoriety for Sherman, and on the strength of it a small reservoir of Western curiosities has been established there.

I went over to the curiosity ranche while the train was taking breath, to see what I could see and buy it if the price were not too high.

There were a great many Western curiosities from various parts of the country, and I got deeply interested in them.

I love to find some old relic of ancient times or some antique weapon of warfare peculiar to the noble Aztecs. I can ponder over them by the hour and enjoy it first-rate.

Among the living wonders I noticed a bale of Indian arrows. These arrows are beautiful to look upon, and are remarkably well preserved. They are as good as new. I asked, simply as a matter of form, if they were Indian arrows. The man said they were. Then I asked who made them, and he got mad and wouldn't speak to me.

I do not think I am unreasonable to want to know who makes my Indian arrows, am I?

I am willing to pay a fair price for the genuine Connecticut made arrow with cane shaft, and warranted cast steel point, but the Indian arrow made at Omaha is not durable.

This curiosity man would make more money and command a larger trade if he were not so quick-tempered.

He had also some Western cactus as a curiosity for the tenderfoot who had never fooled with a cactus much.

It was the clear thing, however. I sat down on one to test its genuineness. It stood the test better than I did. When you have doubts about a cactus and don't know whether it is a genuine cactus or a young watermelon with its hair banged, you can test it by sitting down on it. It may surprise you at first, but it tickles the cactus almost to death.

For a high-priced house plant and gentle meek-eyed exotic that don't care much for affection, the Rocky Mountain cactus takes the cake.

It is very easy to live, and don't require much fondling. It will enjoy life better if you will get mad at it about once a week and pull it up by the roots, and kick it around the yard. Water it carefully every four years; if you water it oftener than that, it will be surprised, and gradually pine away and die.

Another item I must not forget in giving directions for the cultivation of this rare tropical plant: get some one to sit down on it occasionally—if you don't feel equal to it yourself. There's nothing that makes a cactus thrive and flourish so much as to have a victim with linen pants on, sit down on it and then get up impulsively like. If a cactus can have these little attentions bestowed upon it, it will live to a good old age, and insinuate itself through the pantaloons of generations yet unborn. Plant in a gravelly, coarse soil, and kick it every time you think of it.

From *Bill Nye and Boomerang.*

Circular from Colorow

Office of Chief Mutilator, May 1, 1881

To all to whom these presents may come, greeting:

It is my desire and aim, this summer, to make the Ute picnic season for 1881 the most successful ever known in history. Arrangements have been made by which comfort and convenience will be added to the opportunity to see some of the most delightful scenery in Colorado.

I desire, therefore, the entire co-operation of all our people, and will spare no pains necessary to make the excursion one long to be remembered by those who survive.

I wish to secure as large a campaign fund as possible, and therefore ask those who read this circular to contribute $50 each to assist in defraying the expenses of the grand farewell tour of Colorado. This sum is very small when we consider the amount of unadulterated hilarity we will have.

Among the attractive features of the approaching season will be a supply of canned fruit, Boston baked beans, picnic crackers and lemons.

We shall also carry a better grade of whisky than on former trips of this kind.

There will, of course, be dull days when we cannot well go out of camp, and when, of course, we cannot kill anybody. To do away with the *ennui* of such days, we will have with us a well selected stock of agricultural reports, and patent office reports, which some one of the party will read aloud to the rest.

Some new styles of torture for prisoners taken on the trip, will also be introduced this season, which will not only prolong the exercises, but give a much higher grade of entertainment to everyone than heretofore.

In addition to the mirth-provoking farce of roasting Colorado people over a sage-brush fire, we will introduce the side-splitting comedy entitled "Starvation made easy, or Dr. Tanner in the Rocky mountains."

The victims will be picked up on the various ranches of Colorado.

Children will not be wasted as formerly, but those not worked up into pot pie along the road will be canned for winter use.

In looking over and assorting game after the day's sport, bald-headed men will be fed to the coyotes, after their pockets have been assayed.

A prize for the largest number of scalps obtained during the excursion will be awarded, consisting of a gold-headed cane; second highest number, one year's paid up subscription to the *Daily Boomerang*; third highest number, handsome portrait of Anna Dickinson as "Hamlet."

In the above award no bald-headed scalps will be counted. Scalps must be in a good state of preservation, and properly tanned, with the fur on.

To the member of the excursion stealing the largest number of horses and ponies, a fashionable suit of clothes, consisting of a gold collar-button, will be given.

At the scalp dances, this season, there will be but little change in party dresses. A swallow-tail coat of red paint, with trimming of ranch butter, will be the *récherché* thing for the cooler months, and during July and August the paint will be omitted.

The new racquet scalp dance will be very popular this season, and will be just too sweet.

The Ute German will be abolished; also all other Germans found along the route.

The utmost harmony and unity of purpose is urged by the Chief Mutilator, as we desire that the coming summer shall give the New Jerusalem a bigger boom in immortalized ranchmen than the history of the world has ever known.

William H. Colorow
Chief Mutilator

O. Snockemonthegob,
    Acting Custodian of Valley Tan

From *Forty Liars and Other Lies.*

The Plug Hat in Wyoming

Perhaps no evidence of an advanced stage of mental culture and social superiority has been received in Wyoming with more marked coolness and disfavor than the plug hat. This intolerance is not easily accounted for; but there are several causes which may indirectly touch upon the subject under discussion.

In the first place, the climate of Wyoming is not congenial to the plug hat. You may wear one at 1 o'clock with impunity, if you can dodge the vigilance committee, and at three minutes past 1 a little cat's paw of wind will come sighing down from the Snowy Range, that makes the cellars and drive-wells tremble, and the hat looks like a frightened picket fence.

It is not pleasant for a stranger to wear a plug hat in Wyoming, because the police and other officers of the law look upon him with suspicion; but he can wear out this feeling if he leads an upright life. The climate, however, is something that he cannot wear out. You can wear a hole in your pantaloons if you wish, or you can dress up in chapparejos and a yellow necktie, without attracting much attention; but when you put on a plug hat, the hoodlum and the elements are against you.

We wore a plug hat here one whole day once. It was not a very large or heavy hat, but before night it seemed to weigh a ton, and it felt as large as a bass drum.

The air of Wyoming, when it is feeling pretty well, will wear out a plug hat in about two hours, and leave it looking like a joint of iron stovepipe. When the atmosphere is full of geological specimens, and blossom rock, and deceased tom cats, it is not a good time to wear the plug hat. At the first sign of the wind the hat gets fuzzy, like the corset of a bumble bee. Then some more little whispering zephyrs come along from the same bed of violets on

Vinegar Hill, and after that man has followed his hat for fifteen or twenty miles as the crow flies, he picks it out of a bunch of sage-brush, and it is as bald-headed as a door-knob.

In former years they used to hang a man who wore a plug hat west of the Missouri, but after a while they found that it was a more cruel and horrible punishment to let him wear it, and chase it over the foothills when the frolicsome breeze caught it up and toyed with it, and lammed it against the broad brow of Laramie Peak.

An old hunter was out among the Black Hills, east of town, last summer, hunting for cotton-tails and sage-hens, and he ran across a little gulch where the abrupt rocks closed together and formed a little atmospheric eddy, so to speak. There in that lonely reservoir he found what he at first considered a petrified hat store. It was a genuine deposit of escaped straw hats and plug hats that the frolic-some zephyrs had caught up and carried for ten miles, until this natural hat-rack had secured them. Of course there were other articles of apparel, and some debilitated umbrellas, but the deposit seemed to assay mostly hats.

Time may overcome at last the public disfavor, but until the Rocky Mountain wind is lulled to repose, so that a plug hat will not have to be tied on with a wrought iron stair-rod, the soft hat will be the prevailing style of roof.

From *Forty Liars and Other Lies.*

How They Salt a Claim

"I wish you would explain to me all about this salting of claims that I hear so much about," said a meek-eyed tenderfoot to a grizzly old miner who was panning about six ounces of pulverized quartz. "I don't see what they want to salt a claim for, and I don't understand how they do it."

"Well, you see, a hot season like this they have to salt the claim lots of times to keep it. A fresh claim is good enough for a fresh tenderfoot, but the old timers won't look at anything but a pickled claim. You know what quartz is, probably?"

"No."

"Well, every claim has quartz. Some more and some less. You find out how many quartz there are and then put in so many pounds of salt to the quart. Wildcat claims require more salt, because the wildcat spoils quicker than anything else.

"Sometimes you catch a sucker, too, and you have to put him in brine or you lose him. That's one reason why they salt a claim.

"Then again, you often grub stake a man"—

"But what is a grub stake?"

"Well, a grub stake is a stake that the boys hang their grub on so they can carry it. Lots of mining men have been knocked cold by a blow from a grub stake.

"What I wanted to say, though, was this: you will probably at first strike free milling poverty, with indications of something else. Then you will, no doubt, sink till you strike bedrock, or a true fissure gopher hole, with traces of disappointment.

"That's the time to put in your salt. You can shoot it into the shaft with a double-barreled shotgun, or wet it and apply it with a whitewash brush. If people turn up their noses at your claim then, and say it is a snide, and that they think there is something rotten in Denmark, you can tell them that they are clear off, and that you have salted your claim, and that you know it is all right."

The last seen of the tenderfoot, he was buying a double-barreled shotgun and ten pounds of rock salt.

There's no doubt but a mining camp is the place to send a young man who wants to acquire knowledge and fill his system full of information that will be useful to him as long as he lives.

From *Forty Liars and Other Lies.*

Women Wanted

As the result of the publication of an article in these columns some time ago under the above head, a perfect deluge of letters has been turned loose upon the office from women all over the country who evidently mistook the drift of the editorial upon Wyoming's want.

Instead of answering all these letters separately and personally, which would be utterly impossible without nine stenographers and twenty-seven coarsehand writers, we wish to say that the original statement was correct and written in deadly earnest.

Wyoming wants women, and wants them bad, but there is no very clamorous demand for sentimental fossils who want a bonanza husband and a pass from the effete east.

This paragraph probably puts the kibosh on about 75 per cent of those who have written us so far.

A young and rapidly growing territory is of course largely populated by men, but they are not as a rule millionaires with a bad cough. Most of them are healthy and still retain their mental faculties. That is the reason they do not care to import a horde of weak-minded gushers and turn them loose upon a thriving municipality.

One soft-eyed hyena who has no doubt been ignored for thirty years, writes us a poetical epistle which ought to melt a more obdurate heart than ours. It is written on six pages of foolscap in violet ink and blank verse. Every word has an ornamental tail on it and the t's are crossed with a delicate hair line that looks like a Saratoga wave on a ball of butter. Her soul goes out to us in thankfulness in a way that has created a coolness in our family which it will take years to efface.

The idea of cooking large red doughnuts in hot lard, or wringing out heavy underclothing in soapsuds and hanging them out in a back yard on a cold day, does not seem to occur to her.

There are very few households here as yet that are able to keep their own private poet. We try to keep up with the onward march of improvement so far as possible, but we are most of us still too gross to give up our meals and gorge ourselves on a stanza of cold poem on the half shell.

The day may come when we will be glad to sacrifice beefsteak for divine afflatus, but it will be some little time before that period is reached.

The crisp, dry air here is such that hunger is the chief style of yearn in Wyoming, and a good cook can get $125 per month, where a bilious poet would be bothered like sin to get a job at $5 per week.

That is the reason we are writing these terse and perhaps ungallant words. We want to discourage the immigration of a large majority of those who have written us on this subject. They are too fresh and too yearnful in their nature. One of them opens a four-column letter to us with these words:

"BOOMERANG, thou has spàke. Thy words hast bursted upon mine ear."

Now if we have been the cause of any such funny business as that, we are sorry and ashamed of it.

We feel that we have done something that we would give $2 to undo.

We wanted to do the territory some good and to encourage a class of women to come to this region who would know enough to construct a buttonhole on an overcoat so that it wouldn't look like the optic of a cross-eyed hog. We wanted to throw out an invitation to womankind to come here and locate, but we did not know that such people as responded classed themselves as women. We do not consider woman a drudge or a slave across the nape of whose neck the overshoe of tyrant man is planted.

A thousand times nay!

We look upon woman, however, as useful in the great struggle of life. Generally she is on one side of the struggle and the tyrant man on the other.

One thing, however, is settled. There is not such a mad rush at present for blank verse makers as there is for women of sound sense who can make a pie that will not taste like a stove lid veneered with cod liver oil.

In using these cruel words, we do it in order to silence this ubiquitous howl on the part of these modest violets who expect to get off the train here and meet a confirmed invalid at the depot with a carriage and a marriage license.

The old man with the hectic flush and a life insurance policy for $150,000 is not at present ransacking the four quarters of the globe for a little rosebud 39 years old who don't know enough to boil a teakettle.

The young lady who thinks that the men of the west don't recognize the genuine article when they see it, is laboring under a temporary delusion. Of course the men who live in Wyoming are heathen as a class, and let their hair grow long and deserve the pity and commiseration of more cultivated people, but they would need a good deal more genuine sympathy if they were linked for all time with some of the timid gazelles who have written us on this subject.

From *Forty Liars and Other Lies.*

A Headlight in View

THE CONDUCTOR'S STORY OF A NIGHT TRAIN ON THE UNION PACIFIC

"Yes," said the conductor, biting off the tip of a cigar and slowly scratching a match on his leg, "I've seen a good deal of railroad life that's interesting and exciting in the twenty years that I've been twisting brakes and slamming doors for a living.

"I've seen all kinds of sorrow and all kinds of joy—seen the happy bridal couple starting out on their wedding tour with the bright and hopeful future before them, and the black-robed mourner on her way to a new-made grave wherein she must bury the idol of her lonely old heart.

"Wealth and pinching poverty ride on the same train, and the merry laugh of the joyous, healthy child is mingled with the despairing sigh of the aged. The great antipodes of life are familiar to the conductor for every day the extremes of the world are meeting beneath his eye.

"I've mutilated the ticket of many a black-leg and handled the passes of our most eminent deadheads. I don't know what walk of life is more crowded with thrilling incidents than mine."

"Ever have any smash-ups?"

"Smash-ups? Oh, yes, several of them. None, however, that couldn't have been a good deal worse.

"There is one incident of my railroad life," continued the conductor, running his tongue carefully over a broken place in the wrapper of his cigar, "that I never spoke of before to anyone. It has caused me more misery and wretchedness than any one thing that ever happened to me in my official career.

"Sometimes even now, after the lapse of many years, I awake in the night with the cold drops of agony standing on my face and the horrible nightmare upon me with its terrible surroundings, as plain as on the memorable night it occurred.

"I was running extra on the Union Pacific for a conductor who was an old friend of mine, and who had gone South on a vacation for his health.

"At about 7:30, as near as I can remember, we were sailing along all comfortable one evening with a straight stretch of track ahead for ten or fifteen miles, running on time and everybody feeling tiptop, as overland travelers do who get acquainted with each other and feel congenial. All at once the train slowed down, ran in on an old siding and stopped.

"Of course, I got out and ran ahead of the engine to see what the matter was. Old Antifat, the engineer, had got down and was on the main track looking ahead to where, twinkling along about six or seven miles down the road, apparently, was the headlight of an approaching train. It was evidently 'wild' for nothing was due that we knew of at that hour.

"However, we had been almost miraculously saved from a frightful wreck by the engineer's watchfulness, and everybody went forward and shook old Antifat by the hand and cried and thanked him till it was the most affecting scene for a while that I ever witnessed. It was as though we had stopped upon the very verge of a bottomless chasm, and everybody was laughing and crying at once, till it was a kind of a cross between a revival and a picnic.

"After we had waited about half an hour, I should say, for the blasted train to come up and pass us, and apparently she was no nearer, a cold, clammy suspicion began to bore itself into the adamantine shell of my intellect. The more I thought of it, the more unhappy I felt. I almost wished that I was dead. Cold streaks ran up my back followed by hot ones. I wanted to go home. I wanted to be where the hungry, prying eyes of the great, throbbing work-day world could not see me.

"I called Antifat one side and said something to him. He swore softly to himself and kicked the ground, and looked at the headlight still glimmering in the distance. Then he got on his engine and I yelled 'All aboard.' In a few moments we were moving again, and the general impression was that the train ahead was side tracked and waiting for us, although there wasn't a side track within twenty miles, except the one we had just left.

"It was never exactly clear to the passengers where we passed that wild train, but I didn't explain it to them. I was too much engrossed with my surging thoughts.

"I never felt my own inferiority so much as I did that night. I never so fully realized what a mere speck man is upon the bosom of the universe.

"When I surveyed the starry vault of heaven and considered its illimitable space, where, beyond and stretching on forever, countless suns are placed as centers, around which solar systems are revolving in their regular orbits, each little world peopled perhaps with its teeming millions of struggling humanity, and then other and mightier systems of worlds revolving about these systems till the mind is dazed and giddy with the mighty thought; and then when I compared all this universal magnificence, this brilliant aggregation of worlds and systems of worlds, with one poor, grovelling worm of the dust, only a little insignificant atom, only a poor, weak, erring, worthless, fallible, blind, groping railroad conductor, with my train peacefully sidetracked in the gathering gloom and patiently waiting for the planet Venus to pass on the main track, there was something about the whole somber picture that has over-shadowed my whole life and made me unhappy, and wretched while others were gay.

"Sometimes Antifat and myself meet at some liquid restaurant and silently take something in memory of our great sorrow, but never mention it. We never tear open the old rankling wound or laugh over the night we politely gave the main track to Venus while we stood patiently on the siding."

From *Forty Liars and Other Lies.*

Our Compliments

We have nothing more to say of the editor of the Sweetwater *Gazette*. Aside from the fact that he is a squint-eyed, consumptive liar, with a breath like a buzzard and a record like a convict, we don't know anything against him. He means well enough, and if he can evade the penitentiary and the vigilance committee for a few more years, there is a chance for him to end his life in a natural way. If he don't tell the truth a little more plentifully, however, the Green River people will rise as one man and churn him up till there won't be anything left of him but a pair of suspenders and a wart.

From *Forty Liars and Other Lies*.

The Mania for Marking Clothes by Fred Opper

Mania for Marking Clothes

"The most quiet, unobtrusive man I ever knew," said Buck Bramel to a BOOMERANG man, "was a young fellow who went into North Park in an early day from the Salmon river. He was also reserved and taciturn among the miners, and never made any suggestions if he could avoid it. He was also the most thoughtful man about other people's comfort I ever knew.

"I went into the cabin one day where he was lying on the bed, and told him I had decided to go into Laramie for a couple of weeks to do some trading. I put my valise down on the floor and was going out, when he asked me if my clothes were marked. I told him that I never marked my clothes. If the washerwoman wanted to mix up my wardrobe with that of a female seminary, I would have to stand it, I supposed.

"He thought I ought to mark my clothes before I went away, and said he would attend to it for me. So he took down his revolver and put three shots through the valise.

"After that a coolness sprang up between us, and the warm friendship that had existed so long was more or less busted. After that he marked a man's clothes over in Leadville in the same way, only the man had them on at the time. He seemed to have a mania on that subject, and as they had no insanity experts at Leadville in those days, they thought the most economical way to examine his brain would be to hang him, and then send the brain to New York in a baking powder can.

"So they hung him one night to the bough of a sighing mountain pine.

"The autopsy was, of course, crude; but they sawed open his head and scooped out the brain with a long handled spoon and sent it on to New York. By some mistake or other it got mixed up with some sample specimens of ore from 'The Brindle Tom Cat' discovery, and was sent to the assayer in New York instead of the insanity smelter and refiner, as was intended.

"The result was that the assayer wrote a very touching and grieved letter to the boys, saying that he was an old man anyway, and he wished they would consider his gray hairs and not try to palm off their old groceries on him. He might have made errors in his assays, perhaps—all men were more or less liable to mistakes— but he flattered himself that he could still distinguish between a piece of blossom rock and a can of decomposed lobster salad, even if it was in a baking-powder can. He hoped they would not try to be facetious at his expense any more, but use him as they would like to be treated themselves when they got old and began to totter down toward the silent tomb.

"This is why we never knew to a dead moral certainty, whether he was O.K. in the upper story, or not."

From *Baled Hay*.

The Woes of a One-Legged Man

Yesterday morning, while the main guy of *The Boomerang* sanctum was putting some carbolic acid in the paste pot, and unlimbering his genius, and tuning his lyre preparatory to yanking loose a few stanzas on the midsummer cucumber, a man with a cork leg, and the chastened air of one who is second lieutenant in the home circle under the able and efficient command of his wife, came softly in and sat down on a volume containing the complete poems of Noah Webster.

He waited patiently till he could catch the eye of the speaker, humming softly to himself—

> "Green grows the grave by the wild, dashing river,
>   Where sleeps the brave with his arrow and quiver."

When the time had arrived for the lodge to open up unfinished business, communications and new business, he ran his wooden leg through the rounds of a chair and said:

"I desire to make a few remarks on the subject of home government, and the rights a husband may have which his wife is bound to respect."

"Yes; but we don't enter the family circle with our all-pervading influence. We simply attack evils of a public or general nature. You should pour your tale of woe into the ears of an attorney. He will dish out the required balm to you at so much per balm."

"I know, but this is not strictly a case for the courts. It's a case which raises the question of the husband's priority, and agitates the whole social fabric.

"Last week I celebrated my 43rd birthday, or I started to celebrate it, and circumstances over which I had no control arose and

85

busted the programme, as mapped out by the committee of arrangements.

"It was the intention of the party, consisting of myself and several others of our most eminent men, to go over to Sybille canyon with a mountain wagon and a pair of pinto plugs for a little wholesome recreation. We had some weapons for slaying the frolicsome jack rabbit and the timid sage hen, and had provided ourselves against every possible rattlesnake contingency also. We had taken more precautions in this direction, perhaps, than in any other way, and were in shape to enjoy the wild grandeur of the eternal hills without fear from the poisonous reptile of the rugged gulches and alkali bottoms of this picturesque western country.

"We were all loaded up in good shape for the trip and drove around to my house to get a camp kettle and some lemons. I went into the pantry to get a couple of pounds of sugar and a nutmeg. My wife met me in the pantry and roughly and brutally smelled of my breath.

"This was not the prerogative of a true wife, but she weighs 200 and is middling resolute, so I allowed her to do so, although every man's breath is his own property, and if he allows his wife to take advantage of her marital vows to smell his breath on the most unlooked for occasions, what is to become of our boasted freedom?

"I then went up stairs into a closet after a lap robe and a pillow to use in case any of us got sunstruck.

"My wife came in just then, and as I started away with the pillow, she tripped me up so I fell inside the closet, and before I could recover from my surprise, she sat down on me in such a solemn and impressive manner that my eyes hung out on my cheeks like the bronze door knobs on a Pullman car.

"There I was in the impenetrable gloom of a closet, with the trusting companion of my homelife flattening out my stomach till I could feel my watch chain against my spinal column. She then unscrewed my cork leg in a mechanical kind of a way and locked it up in the bureau drawer, putting the key in her pocket.

"After that she fastened the closet door on the outside, and told the party that I would be unable, owing to the inclemency of the weather, to take part in the exercises at Sybille canyon.

"All through that long, long weary day, I stood around on one leg and looked out of the window, thinking what a potent spell is exerted over the wooden-legged man by an able-bodied wife.

"It is a question, sir, which is of vital interest to us all. Must the one-legged minority continue thus to subserve the interests of the two-legged majority? I ask you, as the representative of the all civilizing, all leveling, all powerful and all jewhillikin press, how long the cork-limbed, taxation-without-representation masses must limp around the house and sew carpet rags, writhing in the death-like grip of a two-legged oligarchy?"

He did not wait for an answer. He simply gathered up a few of our freshest exchanges and stole softly down the stairs.

We decline to make any comment one way or the other, because we do not know that the country is ripe for the discussion of this question, but it deserves cold, calm, candid thought on the part of all thinking men, to say the least.

From *Forty Liars and Other Lies.*

The Woman with the Hose

We have spoken of the garden hose before, but in the former article we were unable to produce the steel engraving that should have gone with it. One of the staff, it seems, had loaned the steel plate to Scribner, of New York, to work into an article on medieval art.

The garden hose has risen within the past few years from comparative obscurity to where it commands the respect and attention of a civilized world. In the hands of a woman who is talking to some one in the house, it becomes an instrument of great potency and uncertainty.

By being on your guard at all times, you may dodge the primeval cow, or the deadly wheelbarrow, but the garden squirt is inevitable and unavoidable.

Death itself may be delayed sometimes by surgical skill and constant care, but the wild, weird moisture of the garden hose is ever lurking near and looking for its victim. It follows a man like the transcript of an old judgment in the district court.

We once knew a man who was successful in business, and surrounded by everything that goes to make life desirable.

He didn't owe anybody and nobody owed him. He owned a handsome residence with velvet lawns, and cast-iron bulldogs on each side of his front steps. He had horses and carriages, with his monogram on the harness, and a large chattel mortgage on the whole thing, and there was nothing that money would buy that he did not have.

But there was a Nemesis camped on his trail. It was in the form of a sad-eyed bilious woman, who lived next door, and who was armed with a garden hose.

She had one glass eye that she couldn't most always rely on, and she wore a large sun bonnet, that had a droop to it like the Chicago cattle market.

This man would catch the direction of the glass eye, and make calculations accordingly, but he generally got bathed in cold water and astonishment. When he wasn't misled by the glass eye, he got fooled by the limber sun bonnet, till finally he got desperate. He gradually became despondent and cynical. When his wife made humorous remarks to him he would not laugh, as he was wont to do. At first she thought he had a boil or something of that kind gnawing at his vitals, but he would not tell her the cause of his woe.

He bore it in silence till the close of the summer, and when the maples were crimsoned with the dying splendor of the autumn, one day they brought him home on a cellar door, and laid him out in the off bed-room with his store clothes on.

Toward the close of a sunny day in autumn the sombre funeral line slowly filed away from the elegant mansion, and as it moved past, there was a loud hiss through the silent air, and a torrent of cold water that drenched the entire procession.

It was the garden hose with its last sad squirt.

From *Forty Liars and Other Lies.*

Table Etiquette

There are a great many people who behave well otherwise, but at table do things that if not absolutely *outre* and *ensemble*, are at least *pianissimo* and *sine die*.

It is with a view to elevating the popular taste and etherealizing, so to speak, the manners and customs of our readers, that we give below a few hints upon table etiquette.

If by writing an article of this kind we can induce one man who now wipes his hands on the table cloth to come up and take higher ground and wipe them on his pants, we shall feel amply repaid.

If you cannot accept an invitation to dinner do not write your regrets on the back of a pool check with a blue pencil. This is now regarded as *ricochet*.

A simple note to your host informing him that your washer-woman refuses to relent is sufficient.

On seating yourself at the table draw off your gloves and put them in your lap under your napkin. Do not put them in the gravy, as it would ruin the gloves and cast a gloom over the gravy. If you have just cleaned your gloves with benzine, you might leave them out in the front yard.

If you happen to drop gravy on your knife blade, back near the handle, do not run the blade down your throat to remove the gravy, as it might injure your epiglottis, and it is not considered *embonpoint*, anyway.

When you are at dinner do not take up a raw oyster on your fork and playfully ask your host if it is dead. Remarks about death at dinner are in very poor taste.

Pears should be held by the stems and peeled gently but firmly, not as though you were skinning a dead horse. It is not *bon ton*.

Oranges are held on a fork while being pulled, and the facetious style of squirting the juice into the eye of your hostess is now *au revoir*.

Stones in cherries or other fruit should not be placed upon the tablecloth, but slid quietly and unostentatiously into the pocket of your neighbor or noiselessly tossed under the table.

If you strike a worm in your fruit do not call attention to it by mashing it with a nut-cracker. This is not only uncouth, but it is regarded in the best society as *blasé* and exceedingly *vice versa*.

Macaroni should be cut into short pieces and eaten with an even graceful motion, not absorbed by the yard.

In drinking wine, when you get to the bottom of your glass do not throw your head back and draw in your breath like the exhaust of a bath tub in order to get the last drop, as it engenders a feeling of the most depressing melancholy among the guests.

After eating a considerable amount do not rise and unbuckle your vest strap in order to get more room, as it is exceedingly *au fait* and *dishabille*.

If by mistake you drink out of your finger bowl, laugh heartily and make some facetious remark which will change the course of conversation and renew the friendly feeling among the members of the party.

Ladies should take but one glass of wine at dinner. Otherwise there might be difficulty in steering the male portion of the procession home.

Do not make remarks about the amount your companion has eaten. If the lady who is your company at table, whether she be your wife or the wife of some one else, should eat quite heartily, do not offer to pay your host for his loss or say to her "Great Scott! I hope you will not kill yourself because you have the opportunity," but be polite and gentlemanly, even though the food supply be cut off for a week.

If one of the gentlemen should drop a raw oyster into his bosom and he should have trouble in fishing it out, do not make facetious remarks about it, but assist him to find it, laughing heartily all the time.

From *Forty Liars and Other Lies.*

The Female Barber

Women are now tackling every profession and style of business. There is hardly a path of life adown whose shaded paths we do not find the young lady sauntering in her charmingly careless manner.

Many of them are becoming barbers, and successful ones, too. There is a gentle touch required by a barber which is very grateful to the victim, and which is easily picked up by the lady apprentice.

There is a nameless joy steals into a man's soul when a musical voice tickles a man's ear as he lies in the chair with his eyes closed, while the tips of rosy fingers take him by the nose and pry open his mouth and a dainty twist of the wrist fills his back teeth full of soap and rain water.

O, woman! Little do you know what a power for good do you possess. When you jab a man's head back against the gable end of the barber chair, and hang it over behind so that his Adam's apple sticks up into the scented air like the breast bone of an old gobbler that has died of starvation, you have the great, manly lord of creation where he is as weak and tractable as a child.

Then you can wear him out with an old razor that you have shaved the whole broad universe with. Then you can peel off one feature after another and throw it into an old nail keg, and while you slice him up into sausage meat you can talk to him and make him think he is having a chunk of luxury ladled out to him such as no other living man ever got.

If a female barber is handsome, she can shave her customers with a bed-slat and powder their faces with Cayenne pepper and giant powder, and it will be all right.

A homely female barber, however, would have nothing to do but to hone up old razors and think about the sombre past.

From *Forty Liars and Other Lies.*

A Word About Wild Sheep

Scribner's Monthly has the following little fragment of information relative to western zoology, which we cheerfully reprint. Not so much on account of its novelty, but for the breezy style in which it is narrated:

"At the base of Sheep Rock, one of the winter strongholds of the Shasta flocks, there lives a stock-raiser, who has the advantage of observing the movements of wild sheep every winter; and in the course of a conversation with him on the subject of their diving habits, he pointed to the front of a lava headland about a hundred and fifty feet high, which is only eight or ten degrees out of the perpendicular. 'There,' said he, 'I followed a band of them fellows to the back of that rock yonder, and expected to capture them all, for I thought I had a dead thing on them. I got behind them on a narrow bench that runs along the face of the wall near the top, and comes to an end where they couldn't get away without falling and being killed; but they jumped off and landed all right as if that were the regular thing with them.'"

We don't wish to rub off the flush and bloom of this story, because we hate to have any one sit down on a favorite lie of ours, but there are little weak places in the above statement. For instance, a mountain sheep has bowels. He uses them in deducting the nutritious properties of the bunch grass and moss agates which he puts into his system. Examination by well known anatomists has shown, that the bowels of the mountain sheep are constructed on the old plan instead of being made of Bessemer steel, with copper rivets and dust-proof brass cap, as is generally supposed.

A fall of 150 feet perpendicularly would mix up the works of a mountain sheep so that he wouldn't know whether he had diphtheria or inflammation of the bowels.

Again, the mountain sheep, like all vertebrates, has a spinal column, something like the editorial column of this paper. The general impression that the backbone of a mountain sheep is made of vulcanized rubber and spiral springs, is incorrect. If he were to jump 150 feet, therefore, toward the center of the earth, something would have to flummix.

The chances are that he would find his lumbar vertebrae in his vest pocket and his gambrel joint jammed through his liver. We do not deny that the mountain sheep has a forehead that is harder to drill a fact through than that of the average spring poet, but his forehead only protects his intellect. It don't prevent his hind legs jamming through his diaphragm when he jumps 150 feet, and strikes on a chunk of prehistoric granite.

We don't want to say anything disrespectful of *Scribner's Monthly*, because it is older than we are, and we want to be respectful to old age; but whenever you find a place where a flock of mountain sheep have jumped down a precipice 150 feet deep, you can go and gather up more giblets of wild mutton than you will use all summer.

From *Forty Liars and Other Lies.*

Bill Nye's Complaint

We hardly ever make trouble where it is possible to avoid it, but we feel that a word or two is necessary relative to the man who delivers coal. We never murmur or repine when coal goes up to where you can't see it for weeks at a time, but we patiently go and get fragments of a neighbor's fence and burn them until the price of coal is more depressed. We do not get mad when, after mortgaging our home and hypothecating our pay for a month in advance, we find that our coal is nothing but a stone quarry with little chunks of slate and refractory blossom rock in it. We just dig out what we can make use of for fuel, and take the rest to stone up the cellar and bang the midnight festive cat.

None of these things make us lower ourself by an outburst of temper; but when the driver of a coal wagon rides upon the scales and has himself weighed so that we will purchase him every time we want a load of fuel, and then comes into the back yard and smashes down the side gate, and drives over the children's cart, and breaks down the clothes line, and upsets the ash barrel, and breaks out the window of the coal house, and puts two tons of coal on top of the coal shovel, and buries the kindling nine feet deep, and kills the cat, and winks at the hired girl, and drives over the pet rooster, and tries to climb a shade tree with his team, and then goes away and leaves both gates open so that there is a cold draft of air and eleven cows passing through the yard, we can not help showing that we are annoyed. . . .

From *Cheyenne Sun*, November 4, 1881.

Entomologist

Come, little boys and girls, and hear me tell about a dog I once owned.

Some dogs are prized for their faithfulness, others for their sagacity, and still others for their beauty. My dog was not noticeable for his faithfulness, because he only clung to me when I did not want him, and when I felt lonely and needed sympathy and deep devotion, he was always away from home.

He was not very sagacious, either. He was always doing things which, in the light of a chastened experience and cooler, calmer afterthought, he bitterly regretted.

Thus his life was a wide waste of shattered ambitions and the ghastly ruins of what he might have been.

Neither did I prize him for his beauty; for he was brindle where there was any hair on him and red where there was none, and he had, at one time, dropped his tail into a camp-kettle of boiling water. So that when he took it out and looked at it sadly, he was surprised to see that it looked like a new sausage.

When visitors came to my camp on the Boomerang Consolidated, and I gave them a lunch, my dog would sit near them and look yearningly at them, and pound the floor with his baldheaded tail, and lick his chops, and follow each mouthful of the lunch with such a hungry, hopeless look, that the visitors wished that they were dead.

When I first went out to the mining camp I did not have any dog. I was not poor enough. After a while, however, by judicious inactivity and my aesthetic love for physical calm, I got poor enough. So that I knew I ought to procure a dog, and thus herald my poverty to the world.

I also desired a constant companion who would share my humble lot and never forsake me.

I secured a dog, which I named Entomologist. Do you know what an entomologist is? He is one who makes large collections of antique bugs and peculiar insects and studies their characteristics and peculiarities.

Entomologist seemed to be entirely wrapped up in his collection of insects, and they were very much attached to him.

He had a good many more insects on hand than he really needed, especially fleas. Entomologist introduced into Slippery Elm Gulch a large, early, purple-top, Swedish flea that had an immense run in camp. Most everybody got some of them.

He was very proud of his collection of singular and peculiar fleas. It was about all that he had to be proud of except his appetite.

Entomologist had a wild, ungovernable desire for food that made him a good deal of trouble. He would keep this unnatural appetite under control for days and weeks together, and then he would yield to it and become its willing slave again.

He would eat too much during the day, and at night he would creep into my tent and fill the air with his vain regrets.

I used to try every way to make him overcome his corroding grief, and at last I got to throwing pick-handles and drills, and pack-saddles, and large chunks of specimen quartz and carboniferous profanity at him in the night, to see if I couldn't convince him that it was better to suffer on in silence and smother his woe than to give way to such wild and robust grief.

One night he did not come home, and I feared that he had fallen down the shaft into the lower level of the Boomerang. I found him, however, down at Dobe Abraham's trying to eat a twenty-five foot rawhide lariat.

It seems that he had swallowed fifteen feet of it before he discovered that the other end was tied in a hard knot to an iron picket-pin. When he discovered this, he had moved to reconsider but the motion was defeated. I untied the lariat, however, and let Entomologist swallow it and go home. Then I went to the owner and purchased the lariat. I had one at home just like it, but I thought that it would be as well for Entomologist to have one of his own. I would do anything for my dog. I did not wish to neglect him while he was alive, for I knew I would regret it some day, if he were to be taken from me.

One day in the mellow autumn I went over to town to purchase grub for winter, and took Entomologist with me. He ran around a good deal, and tasted of almost everything; but he knew his weakness, and did not yield to it at first. Finally he found some soft plaster of Paris that had just been mixed near a new house. He had eaten a good many things, but he had never tasted plaster before, so he ate what there was.

It was the effect of a blind impulse, and not the result of Entomologist's more mature judgment. Ah, how rashly the best of us sometimes fly into the face of Providence, and in later years we struggle in tears and agony of spirit to overcome the foolish action of an unguarded moment!

That's the way it was with Entomologist. Five minutes after he ate that plaster he felt as though years of integrity and self-denial could not overcome this rash act.

He lost his old vivacity, and never came up to me any more to lick my face with his warm, damp tongue, or put his cold, wet nose in my ear and sneeze, as he was wont to do when he was well. He gradually lost all interest in his fleas, and allowed them to shift for themselves.

Although he did not moan or complain, I could see that little Entomologist was climbing the golden stair.

One day, just as the sun was lighting up the west and glorifying the horizon with its royal coloring, Entomologist rolled himself up into a small globular wad and died.

*   *   *   *   *

He died without a struggle, but I always knew that he would die easy. If it hadn't been easy he wouldn't have done it. He never would do anything that was difficult, or that required a struggle.

As I write these lines, memory takes me back to those days of the long ago; and while the scalding tear wells up anon to my eyelids and falls upon the page before me, a large paper-weight, white and symmetrical, is lying by my side, and on it is written:

"Plaster cast of Entomologist, taken by himself, (interior view.)
He bit off more than he could chew."

From *Forty Liars and Other Lies.*

Wilting a Lion

Many years ago, when the country was new and infested with the grizzly bear and the prairie dog, there used to be a couple of mountain lions at the Green River eating house. They were kept in a big iron cage at the east end of the platform, and the average tourist was regaled each day by their ferocious antics.

After awhile Cap Lang, who kept the house, got tired of the mountain lions, and traded them to a traveling circus for an old and highly respected African lion with false teeth. He was thoroughly under subjection, and had got so docile that he didn't draw any more as a man-eater for the circus, and they had to feed him Cayenne pepper and turpentine to make him scare the women and children on the front seats, in the greatest living aggregation on earth, and only boss double-hump dromedary and ten-elephant show in the known world.

Still, he was obedient, and when the lion-tamer would pound on the floor of the cage with his foot, the venerable old fraud would open his mouth till you could throw a cook-stove into it, and he would gnash his store teeth and roar till the center-pole would tremble, and pink lemonade would go up to ten cents a glass.

Well, Cap Lang established the king of beasts in his new quarters, and by feeding him hotel soup and chopped feed, with a sprinkling of Cayenne pepper and ground mustard, continued to make him lively enough to give the overland passengers fifty cents' worth of roar after each meal.

Ira Carrington, who used to brake on the passenger between Laramie and Green River, was also a western curiosity. He didn't work for the company so much on account of the salary as he did for the fun he had lying to the tenderfoot. If the pay-car didn't catch him regularly he didn't care much, but if he failed to pick up a victim every trip and fill him full of the wild and gory west, he went home hurt and despondent.

One day he ran across a passenger in the day-coach who was a professional lion-tamer from away back. He admitted that he could paralyze an African lion with the cold and cruel glare of his baleful eye. He had met the king of beasts in his tropical home, and wilted him hundreds of times with his double-barrel glitter.

Mr. Carrington then said that when the train got to Green River there would be an opportunity for him to turn loose on a ferocious brute at the hotel. The news rapidly spread among the passengers that a lion-tamer from Timbuctoo was on board who would, on reaching Green River, give a free performance, in which he would enter the cage and pull the lion's tail out by the roots and throw the bob-tail king of beasts over the eating house.

When the train arrived at Green River the lion-tamer, with his coat off and a blue cotton handkerchief tied around his head, walked up to the cage with his cruel eye fixed on the lion in a reproachful way calculated to fill the ferocious monster with remorse.

The entire load of passengers stood near with bated breath, wondering whether the brave man would cow the haughty king of the forest or get himself chewed up into Vienna sausages.

At this moment Mr. Carrington, who knew the characteristics of the feeble old circus lion of the present day, pounded on the platform with his foot in a loud and boisterous manner, and the king of beasts responded in a way that did great credit to himself and scared the passengers half to death. He opened his mouth so that you could see the basement of his liver, and lashing the cage with his tail, let off a bass solo that pretty near shattered the blue vault of heaven. The hot, fiery breath of the monster came thick and steaming against the cheek of the bold lion-tamer. The red gums and fiery eyes of the mad brute gleamed close to the bars of his cage. The lion-tamer forgot about casting a withering glitter on the lion. In the hurry and excitement it escaped his mind.

Backing slowly away from the cage in order that the king of the forest might recover from his fright, the lion-tamer fell off into a bunch of sage brush. The crowd then greeted him with round after round of applause. Mr. Carrington took him by the suspenders and rescued him.

The lion-tamer then went into the car. He had no business particularly in the car, but he went in there so that he could be away from the prying eyes of the passengers.

This shows how a truly brave man shuns the approbation and applause of the multitude, and also how a bass-wood lion stuffed with baled hay and fitted out with plaster of paris teeth and a heavy baritone voice can out-glare an able-bodied lion-tamer from Kalamazoo.

From *Forty Liars and Other Lies*.

Obituary for Captain Jack

Many of our people have been pained to hear of the sudden death of Captain Jack, of the Ute nation, and none more so than the writer of this.

He was sick but a short time, and even he hardly realized that he was going to die. It is said that five minutes before his demise he was strong and well. In fact, he was a man of unusually strong physique and had a digestion like a corn-sheller. He never felt a pain and rarely employed a physician.

On Saturday last he retired to his tepee, little dreaming that he would be carried out of it in a salt bag.

It seems that he had defied the paleface at the post and in a moment of irritability had killed one of the soldiers. The officer in charge then procured a howitzer and fired a shell into the warrior's tent. This shell, owing to some fault in its construction, no doubt, burst with great havoc near Captain Jack's bosom and a few inches north of his liver. So great was the shock to his system that the only feature that could be recognized was a copper-colored seed wart which he had acquired three years ago.

It was the most severe case of concussion that the history of surgery has ever known. The officer gathered up what could be secured and reported at headquarters the injuries that had been sustained by the great warrior.

While the post surgeon was changing the remains from the salt bag to a baking powder can, Captain Jack breathed his last. His death, however, was not officially announced until a cavalry officer brought in a lobe of liver that he had found in a tree near by. It was then stated authoritatively that Captain Jack was dead. The military department never jumps to conclusions. When a vital organ is found in the limb of a neighboring tree, and the remains under discussion seem to be lacking the particular organ, the military authorities jump at the conclusion that the man is hopelessly injured.

Jack was not educated, but he was great in some respects. He was a self-made man, starting out with no money, no clothes and no friends. He soon, however, acquired distinction as a warrior and a liar which was the envy and admiration of the Ute nation. Now his active brain is still. It has ceased to act. It is congested and scattered over four acres of sage brush.

Still it were better, if he were to die, that he should die in such a manner that we would have no doubts about it. We feel more secure when we know that an Indian has passed away in this manner. Some of his friends, too, may have been cursed through all their lives with the vague fear that Jack had been buried alive. Now it will not be that way. Those who saw his remains will always feel certain that death was instantaneous and painless. His body will lie in state in a cigar box, until the time set for his burial, when he will be interred with proper ceremonies and a corn-planter. We believe that the mountain howitzer is destined at no distant day to become an important factor in the civilization of the Indian and the amelioration of mankind.

From *Laramie Sentinel*, May 6, 1882.

The Stage Bald-Head

Most everyone, who was not born blind, knows that the stage bald-head is a delusion and a snare. The only all-wool, yard-wide bald-head we remember on the American stage, is that of Dunstan Kirke as worn by the veteran Couldock, but Couldock wears his the most. It is the most worn anyhow.

What we started out to say, is, that the stage bald-head and the average stage whiskers make us weary with life. The stage bald-head is generally made of the internal economy of a cow, dried so that it shines, and cut to fit the head as tightly as a potato sack would naturally fit a billiard cue. It is generally about four shades whiter than the red face of the wearer, or *vice versa*. We do not know which is the worst violation of eternal fitness, the red-faced man who wears a deathly white bald-head, or the pale young actor who wears a florid roof on his intellect. Sometimes in starring through the country and playing ten or fifteen hundred engagements, a bald-head gets soiled. We notice that when a show gets to Laramie the chances are that the bald-head of the leading old man is so soiled that he really needs a sheep-dip shampoo. Another feature of this accessory of the stage is its singular failure to fit. It is either a little short at both ends, or it hangs over the skull in large festoons, and wens and warts, in such a way as to make the audience believe that the wearer has dropsy of the brain.

You can never get a stage bald-head near enough like nature to fool the average house-fly. A fly knows in two moments whether it is the genuine, or only a base imitation, and the bald-head of the theatre fills him with nausea and disgust. Nature, at all times hard to imitate, preserves her bald head as she does her sunny skies and deep blue seas, far beyond the reach of the weak, fallible, human imitator. Baldness is like fame, it cannot be purchased. It must be acquired. Some men may be born bald, some may acquire baldness, and others may have baldness thrust upon them, but they generally acquire it.

The stage beard is also rather dizzy, as a rule. It looks as much like a beard that grew there, as a cow's tail would if tied to the bronze dog on the front porch. When you tie a heavy black beard on a young actor, whose whole soul would be churned up if he smoked a full-fledged cigar, he looks about as savage as a bowl of mush and milk struck with a club.

From *Baled Hay*.

Apostrophe Addressed to O. Wilde

[Oscar Wilde lectured in the United States in 1882.]

Soft eyed seraphic kuss
With limber legs and lily on the side,
We greet you from the raw
And uncouth West.

The cowboy yearns to yank thee
To his brawny breast and squeeze
Thy palpitating gizzard
Through thy vest.

Come to the mountain fastness,
Oscar, with thy low neck shirt
And high neck pants;
Fly to the coyote's home,
Thou son of Albion,
James Crow bard and champion aesthete
From o'er the summer sea.

Sit on the fuzzy cactus, king of poesy,
And song,
Ride the fierce broncho o'er the dusty plain
And let the zephyr sigh among thy buttery looks.

Welcome thou genius of dyspeptic song,
Thou bilious lunatic from far-off lands.
Come to the home of genius,
By the snowy hills,
And wrestle with the alcoholic inspiration
Of our cordial home.
    We yearn
To put the bloom upon thy alabaster nose,
And plant jim-jams
In thy clustering hair.
Hail, mighty snoozer from across the main!

We greet thee
With our free, untutored ways and wild,
Peculiar style of deadly beverage.
Come to the broad, free West and mingle
With our high-toned mob.

Come to the glorious Occident
And dally with the pack-mule's whisk-broom tail;
Study his odd yet soft demeanor,
And peculiar mien.

Tickle his gambrel with a sunflower bud
And scoot across the blue horizon
To the tooness of the sweet and succulent beyond.

We'll gladly
Gather up thy shattered remnants
With a broom and ship thee to thy beauteous home.
Forget us not,
Thou bilious pelican from o'er the sea.
Thou blue-nosed clam
With pimply, bulging brow, but
Come and we will welcome thee
With ancient omelet and fragrant sausage
Of forgotten years.

From *Chestnuts*; also in *Forty Liars and Other Lies*.

The Western "Chap"

Few know how voraciously we go for anything in the fashion line. Many of our exchanges are fashion magazines, and nothing is read with such avidity as these highly pictorial aggregations of literature. If there are going to be any changes in the male wardrobe this winter, it behooves us to know what they are. We intend to do so. It is our high prerogative and glorious privilege to live in a land of information. If we do not provide ourself with a few, it is our own fault. Man has spanned the ocean with an electric cable, and runs his street cars with another cable that puts people out of their misery as quick as a giant-powder caramel in a man's chest-protector, under certain circumstances. Science has done almost everything for us, except to pay our debts without leaning toward repudiation. We are making rapid strides in the line of progression. That is, the scientists are. Every little while you can hear a scientist burst a basting thread off his overalls, while making a stride.

It is equally true that we are marching rapidly along in the line of fashion. Change, unceasing change, is the war cry, and he who undertakes to go through the winter with the stage costumes of the previous winter, will find, as Voltaire once said, that it is a cold day.

We look with great concern upon the rapid changes which a few weeks have made. The full voluptuous swell and broad cincha of the shaparajo have given place to the tight pantaletts with feathers on them, conveying the idea that they cannot be removed until death, or an earthquake shall occur.

"Chaps," as they are vulgarly called, deserve more than a passing notice. They are made of leather with fronts of dog-skin with the hair on. The inside breadths are of calf or sheepskin, made plain, but trimmed down the side seam with buckskin bugles and oil-tanned bric-a-brac of the time of Michael Angelo Kelley. On the front are plain pockets used for holding the ball programme and the "pop." The pop is a little design in nickel and steel, which is often used as an inhaler. It clears out the head, and leaves the nasal passages and phrenological chart out on the sidewalk, where pure air is abundant. "Chaps" are rather attractive while the wearer is on horseback, or walking toward you, but when he chassés and "all waltz to places," you discern that the seat of the garment has been postponed sine die. This, at first, induces a pang in the breast of the beholder. Later, however, you become accustomed to the barren and perhaps even stern demeanor of the wearer. You gradually gain control of yourself and master your raging desire to rush up and pin the garment together. The dance goes on. The elite take an adult's dose of ice-cream and other refreshments; the leader of the mad waltz glides down the hall with his mediaeval "chaps," swishing along as he sails; the violin gives a last shriek; the superior fiddle rips the robe of night wide open, with a parting bzzzzt; the mad frolic is over, and $5 have gone into the dim and unfrequented freight depot of the frog-pond-environed past.

From *Baled Hay.*

Accepting the Laramie Postoffice

Office of *Daily Boomerang*, Laramie City, Wy., Aug. 9, 1882.

My dear General.—I have received by telegraph the news of my nomination by the President and my confirmation by the Senate, as postmaster at Laramie, and wish to extend my thanks for the same.

I have ordered an entirely new set of boxes and postoffice outfit, including new corrugated cuspidors for the lady clerks.

I look upon the appointment, myself, as a great triumph of eternal truth over error and wrong. It is one of the epochs, I may say, in the Nation's onward march toward political purity and perfection. I do not know when I have noticed any stride in the affairs of state, which so thoroughly impressed me with its wisdom.

Now that we are co-workers in the same department, I trust that you will not feel shy or backward in consulting me at any time relative to matters concerning postoffice affairs. Be perfectly frank with me, and feel perfectly free to just bring anything of that kind right to me. Do not feel reluctant because I may at times appear haughty and indifferent, cold or reserved. Perhaps you do not think I know the difference between a general delivery window and a three-m quad, but that is a mistake.

My general information is far beyond my years.

With profoundest regard, and a hearty endorsement of the policy of the President and the Senate, whatever it may be,

I remain, sincerely yours,
BILL NYE, P.M.
GEN. FRANK HATTON, Washington, D.C.

From *Remarks By Bill Nye.*

A Fire at a Ball

Down at Gunnison last week a large, select ball was given in a hall, one end of which was partitioned off for sleeping rooms. A young man who slept in one of these rooms, and who felt grieved because he had not been invited, and had to roll around and suffer while the glad throng tripped the light bombastic toe, at last discovered a knot-hole in the partition through which he could watch the giddy multitude. While peeping through the knot-hole, he discovered that one of the dancers, who had an aperture in the heel of his shoe and another in his sock to correspond, was standing by the wall with the ventilated foot near the knot-hole. It was but the work of a moment to hold a candle against this exposed heel until the thick epidermis had been heated red hot. Then there was a wail that rent the battlements above and drowned the blasts of the music. There was a wild scared cry "fire," a frightened throng rushing hither and thither, and then, where mirth and music and rum had gladdened the eye and reddened the cheek a moment ago, all was still save the low convulsive titter of a scantily clad man, as he lay on the floor of his donjon tower and dug his nails in the floor.

From *Baled Hay*.

Fruit

A class of croakers that one meets with everywhere, have steadily maintained that fruit cannot be raised in this Territory. In conversation with a small boy yesterday, we learned that this is not true. It is very simple and easy to do so, even in this rigorous climate. He showed us how it is done. He has a small and delicately constructed harpoon with a tail to it—the apparatus attached to a long string. He goes into the nearest market, and while the clerk is cutting out some choice steaks for the man with the store teeth, the boy throws his harpoon and hauls in on the string. In this way he raises all kinds of fruit, not only for his own use, but he has some to sell. He showed us some that he raised. It was as good as any of the fruit that we buy here, only that there was a little hole on one side, but that don't hurt the fruit for immediate use. He "puts some down," but he don't can or dry any. He says that he applies his where he feels the worst. When he feels as though a Greening or a Bellflower would help him, he goes out and picks it. He showed us a string with a grappling hook attached, on which he had raised a bushel of assorted fruits this fall, and it wasn't a very good string, either.

From *Baled Hay*.

The Mimic Stage by Fred Opper

The Mimic Stage

At the performance of "The Phoenix" here, the other night, there was a very affecting place where the play is transferred very quickly from a street scene to the elegant apartments of Mr. Blackburn, the heavy villain. The street scene had to be raised out of the way, and the effect of the transition was somewhat marred by the reluctance of the scenery in rolling up out of the way. It got about half way up, and stopped there in an undecided manner, which annoyed the heavy villain a good deal. He started to make some blood-curdling remarks about Mr. Bludsoe, and had got pretty well warmed up when the scenery came down with a bang on the stage. The artist who pulls up the curtain and fills the hall lamps, then pulled the scene up so as to show the villain's feet for fifteen or twenty minutes, but he couldn't get it any farther. It seemed that the clothes line, by which the elaborate scenery is operated, got tangled up some way, and this caused the delay. After that another effort was made, and this time the street scene rolled up to about the third story of a brick hotel shown in the foreground, and stopped there, while the clarionet and first violin continued a kind of sad tremulo. Then a dark hand, with a wart on one finger and an oriental dollar store ring on another, came out from behind the wings and began to wind the clothes-line carefully around the pole at the foot of the scene. The villain then proceeded with his soliloquy, while the street scene hung by one corner of the street at an angle of about forty-five degrees.

Laramie will never feel perfectly happy until these little hitches are dispensed with. Supposing that at some place in the play, where the heroine is speaking soft and low to her lover and the proper moment has arrived for her to pillow her sunny head upon his bosom, that street scene should fetch loose, and come down with such momentum as to knock the lovers over into the arms of the bass-viol player. Or suppose that in some death-bed act this same scene, loaded with a telegraph pole at the bottom, should settle down all at once in such a way as to leave the deathbed out on the corner of Monroe and Clark streets, in front of a candy store.

Modern stage mechanism has now reached such a degree of perfection that the stage carpenter does not go up on a step ladder, in the middle of a play, and nail the corner of a scene to a stick of 2×4 scantling, while a duel is going on near the step ladder. In all the larger theatres and opera houses, now, they are not doing that way.

Of course little incidents occur, however, even on the best stages, and where the whole thing works all right. For instance, the other day, a young actor, who was kneeling to a beautiful heiress down east, got a little too far front, and some scenery, which was to come together in the middle of the stage to pianissimo music, shut him outside and divided the tableau in two, leaving the young actor apparently kneeling at the foot of a street lamp, as though he might be hunting for a half a dollar that he had just dropped on the sidewalk.

There was a play in New York, not long ago, in which there was a kind of military parade introduced, and the leader of a file of soldiers had his instructions to march three times around the stage to martial music, and then file off at the left, the whole column, of course, following him. After marching once around, the stage manager was surprised to see the leader deliberately wheel, and walk off the stage, at the left, with the whole battalion following at his heels. The manager went to him and abused him shamefully for his haste, and told him he had a mind to discharge him; but the talented hack driver, who thus acted as the military leader, and who had over-played himself by marching off stage ahead of time said:

"Well, confound it, you can discharge me if you want to, but what was a man to do? Would you have me march around three times when my military pants were coming off, and I knew it? Military pride, pomp, parade, and circumstance, are all right; but it can be overdone. A military squadron, detachment, or whatever it is, can make more of a parade, under certain circumstances, than is advertised. I didn't want to give people more show than they paid for, and I ask you to put yourself in my place. When a man is paid three dollars a week to play a Roman soldier, would you have him play the Greek slave? No, sir; I guess I know what I'm hired to play, and I'm going to play it. When you want me to play Adam in the Garden of Eden, just give me my fig leaf and salary enough to make it interesting, and I will try and properly interpret the character for you, or refund the money at the door."

From *Baled Hay*.

Greeley and Rum

When I visit Greeley I am asked over and over again as to the practical workings of woman suffrage in Wyoming, and when I go back to Wyoming I am asked how prohibition works practically in Greeley, Colo. By telling varied and pleasing lies about both I manage to have a good deal of fun, and also keep the two elements on the anxious seat.

There are two sides to both questions, and some day when I get time and have convalesced a little more, I am going to write a large book relating to these two matters. At present I just want to say a word about the colony which bears the name of the Tribune philosopher, and nestles so lovingly at the chilly feet of the Rocky mountains. As I write, Greeley is apparently an oasis in the desert. It looks like a fertile island dropped down from heaven in a boundless stretch of buffalo grass, sage hens and cunning little prairie dogs. And yet you could not come here as a stranger, and within the colonial barbed wire fence, procure a bite of cold rum if you were President of the United States, with a rattlesnake bite as large as an Easter egg concealed about your person. You can, however, become acquainted, if you are of a social nature and keep your eyes open. I do not say this because I have been thirsty these few past weeks and just dropped on the game, as Aristotle would say, but just to prove that men are like boys, and when you tell them they can't have any particular thing, that is the thing they are apt to desire with a feverish yearn. That is why the thirstful man in Maine drinks from the gas fixture; why the Kansas drinkist gets his out of a rain-water barrel, and why other miracles too numerous to mention are performed.

Whisky is more bulky and annoying to carry about in the coat-tail pocket than a plug of tobacco, but there have been cases where it was successfully done. I was shown yesterday a little corner that would hold six or eight bushels. It was in the wash-room of a hotel, and was about half full. So were the men who came there, for before night the entire place was filled with empty whisky bottles of every size, shape and smell. The little fat bottle with the odor of gin and livery stable was there, and the large flat bottle that you get at Evans, four miles away, generally filled with something that tastes like tincture of capsicum, spirits of ammonia and lingering death, is also represented in this great congress of cosmopolitan bottles sucked dry and the cork gnawed half up.

When I came to Greeley, I was still following the course of treatment prescribed by my Laramie City physician, and with the rest, I was required to force down three adult doses of brandy per day. He used to taste the prescription at times to see if it had been properly compounded. Shortly after my arrival here I ran out of this remedy and asked a friend to go and get the bottle refilled. He was a man not familiar with Greeley in its moisture-producing capacity, and he was unable to procure the vile demon in the town for love or wealth. The druggist even did not keep it, and although he met crowds of men with tears in their eyes and breath like a veteran bung-starter, he had to go to Evans for the required opiate. This I use externally, now, on the vagrant dog who comes to me to be fondled and who goes away with his hair off. Central Colorado is full of partially bald dogs who have wiped their wet, cold noses on me, not wisely but too well.

From *Baled Hay*.

Household Recipes

To remove oils, varnishes, resins, tar, oyster soup, currant jelly, and other selections from the bill of fare, use benzine, soap and chloroform cautiously with whitewash brush and garden hose. Then hang on wood pile to remove the pungent effluvia of the benzine.

To clean ceilings that have been smoked by kerosene lamps, or the fragrance from fried salt pork, remove the ceiling, wash thoroughly with borax, turpentine and rain water, then hang on the clothes line to dry. Afterward pulverize and spread over the pie plant bed for spring water.

To remove starch and roughness from flatirons, hold the iron on a large grindstone for twenty minutes or so, then wipe off carefully with a rag. To make this effective, the grindstone should be in motion while the iron is applied. Should the iron still stick to the goods when in use, spit on it.

To soften water for household purposes, put in an ounce of quicklime in a certain quantity of water. If it is not sufficient, use less water or more quicklime. Should the immediate lime continue to remain deliberate, lay the water down on a stone and pound it with a base ball club.

To give relief to a burn, apply the white of an egg. The yolk of the egg may be eaten or placed on the shirt bosom, according to the taste of the person. If the burn should occur on a lady, she may omit the last instruction.

To wash black silk stockings, prepare a tub of lather, composed of tepid rain water and white soap, with a little ammonia. Then stand in the tub till dinner is ready. Roll in a cloth to dry. Do not wring, but press the water out. This will necessitate the removal of the stockings.

If your hands are badly chapped, wet them in warm water, rub them all over with Indian meal, then put on a coat of glycerine and keep them in your pockets for ten days. If you have no pockets convenient, insert them in the pocket of a friend.

An excellent liniment for toothache or neuralgia, is made of sassafras, oil of organum and a half ounce of tincture of capsicum, with half a pint of alcohol. Soak nine yards of red flannel in this mixture, wrap it around the head and then insert the head in a haystack till death comes to your relief.

To remove scars or scratches from the limbs of a piano, bathe the limb in a solution of tepid water and tincture of sweet oil. Then apply a strip of court plaster, and put the piano out on the lawn for the children to play horse with.

Woolen goods may be nicely washed if you put half an ox gall into two gallons of tepid water. It might be well to put the goods in the water also. If the mixture is not strong enough, put in another ox gall. Should this fail to do the work, put in the entire ox, reserving the tail for soup. The ox gall is comparatively useless for soap, and should not be preserved as an article of diet.

From *Baled Hay*.

The Codfish

This tropical bird very seldom wings his way so far west as Wyoming. He loves the sea breezes and humid atmosphere of the Atlantic ocean, and when isolated in this mountain clime, pines for his native home.

The codfish cannot sing, but is prized for his beautiful plumage and seductive color.

The codfish of commerce is devoid of digestive apparatus, and is more or less permeated with salt.

Codfish on toast is not as expensive as quail on toast.

The codfish ball is made of the shattered remains of the adult codfish, mixed with the tropical Irish potato of commerce.

The codfish has a great wealth of glad, unfettered smile. When he laughs at anything, he has that same side waste of mirth and back teeth that Mr. Talmage has. The Wyoming codfish is generally dead. Death, in most cases, is the result of exposure and loss of appetite. No one can look at the codfish of commerce, and not shed a tear. Far from home, with his system filled with salt, while his internal economy is gone, there is an air of sadness and homesickness and briny hopelessness about him that no one can see unmoved.

It is in our home life, however, that the codfish makes himself felt and remembered. When he enters our household, we feel his all pervading presence, like the perfume of wood violets, or the seductive odor of a dead mouse in the piano.

Friends may visit us and go away, to be forgotten with the advent of a new face; but the cold, calm, silent corpse of the codfish cannot be forgotten. Its chastened influence permeates the entire ranch. It steals into the parlor, like an unbidden guest, and flavors the costly curtains and the high-priced lambrequins. It

120

enters the dark closet and dallies lovingly with your swallowtail coat. It goes into your sleeping apartment, and makes its home in your glove box and your handkerchief case.

That is why we say that it is a solemn thing to take the life of a codfish. We would not do it. We would pass him by a thousand times, no matter how ferocious he might be, rather than take his life, and have our once happy home haunted forever by his unholy presence.

From *Baled Hay*.

Table Manners of Children

Young children who have to wait till older people have eaten all there is in the house, should not open the dining-room door during the meal and ask the host if he is going to eat all day. It makes the company feel ill at ease, and lays up wrath in the parents' heart.

Children should not appear displeased with regular courses at dinner, and then fill up on pie. Eat the less expensive food first, and then organize a picnic in the preserves afterward.

Do not close out the last of your soup by taking the plate in your mouth and pouring the liquid down your childish neck. You might spill it on your bosom, and it enlarges and distorts the mouth unnecessarily.

When asked what part of the fowl you prefer, do not say you will take the part that goes over the fence last. This remark is very humorous, but the rising generation ought to originate some new table jokes that will be worthy of the age in which we live.

Children should early learn the use of the fork, and how to handle it. This knowledge can be acquired by allowing them to pry up the carpet tacks with this instrument, and other little exercises, such as the parent mind may suggest.

The child should be taught at once not to wave his bread around over the table, while in conversation, or to fill his mouth full of potatoes, and then converse in a rich tone of voice with some one in the yard. He might get his dinner down his trachea and cause his parents great anxiety.

In picking up a plate or saucer filled with soup or with moist food, the child should be taught not to parboil his thumb in the contents of the dish, and to avoid swallowing soup bones or other indigestible debris.

Toothpicks are generally the last course, and the children should not be permitted to pick their teeth and kick the table through the other exercises. While grace is being said at table, children should know that it is a breach of good breeding to smouge fruit cake just because their parents' heads are bowed down, and their attention for the moment turned in another direction. Children ought not to be permitted to find fault with the dinner, or fool with the cat while they are eating. Boys should, before going to the table, empty all the frogs and grasshoppers out of their pockets, or those insects might crawl out during the festivities, and jump into the gravy.

If a fly wades into your jelly up to his gambrels, do not mash him with your spoon before all the guests, as death is at all times depressing to those who are at dinner, and retards digestion. Take the fly out carefully, with what naturally adheres to his person, and wipe him on the table cloth. It will demonstrate your perfect command of yourself, and afford much amusement for the company. Do not stand up in your chair and try to spear a roll with your fork. It is not good manners to do so, and you might slip and bust your crust, by so doing. Say "thank you," "much obliged," and "beg pardon," wherever you can work in these remarks, as it throws people off their guard, and gives you an an opportunity to get in your work on the pastry and other bric-a-brac near you at the time.

From *Baled Hay.*

Catching a Buffalo

A pleasing anecdote is being told through the press columns recently, of an encounter on the South Platte, which occurred some years ago between a Texan and a buffalo. The recital sets forth the fact that the Texans went out to hunt buffalo, hoping to get enough for a mess during the day. Toward evening they saw two gentlemen buffalo on a neighboring hill near the Platte, and at once pursued their game, each selecting an animal. They separated at once, Jack going one way galloping after his beast, while Sam went in the other direction. Jack soon got a shot at his game, but the bullet only tore a large hole in the fleshy shoulder of the bull and buried itself in the neck, maddening the animal to such a degree that he turned at once and charged upon horse and rider.

The astonished horse, with the wonderful courage, sagacity and *sang froid* peculiar to the broncho, whirled around two consecutive times, tangled his feet in the tall grass and fell, throwing his rider about fifty feet. He then rose and walked away to a quiet place, where he could consider the matter and give the buffalo an opportunity to recover.

The infuriated bull then gave chase to Jack, who kept out of the way for a few yards only, when, getting his legs entangled in the grass, he fell so suddenly that his pursuer dashed over him without doing him bodily injury. However, as the animal went over his prostrate form, Jack felt the buffalo's tail brush across his face, and rising suddenly, he caught it with a terrific grip and hung to it, thus keeping out of the reach of his enemy's horns, till his strength was just giving out, when Sam hove in sight and put a large bullet through the bull's heart.

This tale is told, apparently, by an old plainsman and scout, who reels it off as though he might be telling his own experience.

An Unequal Match by J. H. Smith

Now, I do not wish to seem captious and always sticking my nose into what is none of my business, but as a logical zoological fact, I desire, in my cursory way, to coolly take up the subject of the buffalo tail. Those who have been in the habit of killing buffaloes, instead of running an account at the butcher shop, will remember that this noble animal has a genuine camel's hair tail about eight inches long, with a chenille tassel at the end, which he throws up into the rarefied atmosphere of the far west, whenever he is surprised or agitated.

In passing over a prostrate man, therefore, I apprehend that in order to brush his face with the average buffalo tail, it would be necessary for him to sit down on the bosom of the prostrate scout and fan his features with the miniature caudal bud.

The buffalo does not gallop a hundred miles a day, dragging his tail across the bunch grass and alkali of the boundless plains.

He snorts a little, turns his bloodshot eyes toward the enemy a moment and then, throwing his cunning little taillet over the dashboardlet, he wings away in an opposite direction.

The man who could lie on his back and grab that vision by the tail would have to be moderately active. If he succeeded, however, it would be a question of the sixteenth part of a second only, whether he had his arms jerked out by the roots and scattered through space or whether he had strength of will sufficient to yank out the withered little frizz and hold the quivering ornament in his hands. Few people have the moral courage to follow a buffalo around over half a day holding on by the tail. It is said that a Sioux brave once tried it, and they say that his tracks were thirteen miles apart. After merrily sauntering around with the buffalo one hour during which time he crossed the territories of Wyoming and Dakota twice and surrounded the regular army three times, he became discouraged and died from the injuries he had received. Perhaps, however, it might have been fatigue.

It might be possible for a man to catch hold of the meager tail of a meteor and let it snatch him through the coming years.

It might be that a man with a strong constitution could catch a cyclone and ride it bareback across the United States and then have a fresh one ready to ride back again, but to catch a buffalo bull in the full flush of manhood, as it were, and retain his tail while he crossed three reservations and two mountain ranges, requires great tenacity of purpose and unusual mental equipoise.

Remember, I do not regard the story I refer to as false, at least I do not wish to be so understood. I simply say that it recounts an incident that is rather out of the ordinary. Let the gentle reader lie down and have a Jack-rabbit driven across his face for instance. The J. Rabbit is as likely to brush your face with his brief and erect tail as the buffalo would be. Then closely attend to the manner in which you abruptly and almost simultaneously have not retained the tail in your memory.

A few people may have successfully seized the grieved and startled buffalo by the tail, but they are not here to testify to the circumstances. They are dead, abnormally and extremely dead.

From *Remarks By Bill Nye.*

The Church Debt

I have been thinking the matter over seriously and I have decided that if I had my life to live over again, I would like to be an eccentric millionaire.

I have eccentricity enough, but I cannot successfully push it without more means.

I have a great many plans which I would like to carry out, in case I could unite the two necessary elements for the production of the successful eccentric millionaire.

Among other things, I would be willing to bind myself and give proper security to any one who would put in money to offset my eccentricity, that I would ultimately die. We all know how seldom the eccentric millionaire now dies. I would be willing to inaugurate a reform in that direction.

I think now that I would endow a home for men whose wives are no longer able to support them. In many cases the wife who was at first able to support her husband comfortably, finally shoulders a church debt, and in trying to lift that she overworks and impairs her health so that she becomes an invalid, while her husband is left to pine away in solitude or dependent on the cold charities of the world.

My heart goes out toward those men even now, and in case I should fill the grave of the eccentric millionaire, I am sure that I would do the square thing by them.

The method by which our wives in America are knocking the church debt silly, by working up their husbands' groceries into "angel food" and selling them below actual cost, is deserving of the attention of our national financiers.

The church debt itself is deserving of notice in this country. It certainly thrives better under a republican form of government than any other feature of our boasted civilization. Western towns spring up everywhere, and the first anxiety is to name the place, the second to incur a church debt and establish a roller rink.

After that a general activity in trade is assured. Of course the general hostility of church and rink will prevent *ennui* and listlessness, and the church debt will encourage a business boom. Naturally the church debt cannot be paid without what is generally known through the West as the "festival and hooraw." This festival is an open market where the ladies trade the groceries of their husbands to other ladies' husbands, and everybody has a "perfectly lovely time." The church clears $2.30, and thirteen ladies are sick all the next day.

This makes a boom for the physicians and later on for the undertaker and general tombist. So it will be seen that the Western town is right in establishing a church debt as soon as the survey is made and the town properly named. After the first church debt has been properly started, others will rapidly follow so that no anxiety need be felt if the church will come forward the first year and buy more than it can pay for.

The church debt is a comparatively modern appliance, and yet it has been productive of many peculiar features. For instance, we call to mind the clergyman who makes a specialty of going from place to place as a successful debt demolisher. He is a part of the general system, just as much as the ice cream freezer or the buttonhole bouquet.

Then there is a row or social knock-down-and-drag-out which goes along with the church debt. All these things add to the general interest, and to acquire interest in one way or another is the mission of the c.d.

I once knew a most exemplary woman who became greatly interested in the wiping out of a church debt, and who did finally succeed in wiping out the debt, but in its last expiring death struggle it gave her a wipe from which she never recovered. She had succeeded in begging the milk and the cream, and the eggs and the sandwiches, and the use of the dishes and the sugar, and the loan of an oyster, and the use of a freezer and fifty button-hole bouquets to be sold to men who were not in the habit of wearing bouquets, but she could not borrow a circular artist to revolve the crank of the freezer, so she agitated it herself. Her husband had to go away prior to the festivities, but he ordered her not to crank the freezer. He had very little influence with her, however, and so to-day he is a widower. The church debt was revived in the following year, and now there isn't a more thriving church debt anywhere in the country. Only last week that church traded off $75 worth of groceries, in the form of asbestos cake and celluloid angel food, in such a way that if the original cost of the groceries and the work were not considered, the clear profit was $13, after the hall rent was paid. And why should the first cost of the groceries be reckoned, when we stop to think that they were involuntarily furnished by the depraved husband and father.

I must add, also, that in the above estimate doctors' bills and funeral expenses are not reckoned.

From *Remarks By Bill Nye.*

Done It A-Purpose

At Greeley a young man with a faded cardigan jacket and a look of woe got on the train, and as the car was a little crowded he sat in the seat with me. He had that troubled and anxious expression that a rural young man wears when he first rides on the train. When the engine whistled he would almost jump out of that cardigan jacket, and then he would look kind of foolish, like a man who allows his impulses to get the best of him. Most everyone noticed the young man and his cardigan jacket, for the latter had arrived at the stage of droopiness and jaded-across-the-shoulders look that the cheap knit jacket of commerce acquires after awhile, and it had shrunken behind and stretched out in front so that the horizon, as you stood behind the young man, seemed to be bound by the tail of this garment, which started out at the pocket with good intentions and suddenly decided to rise above the young man's shoulder blades.

He seemed so different and so frightened among strangers, that I began to talk to him.

"Do you live at Greeley?" I inquired.

"No, sir," he said, in an embarrassed way, as most anyone might in the presence of greatness. "I live on a ranch up the Poudre. I was just at Greeley to see the circus."

I thought I would play the tenderfoot and inquiring pilgrim from the cultured East, so I said: "You do not see the circus often in the West, I presume, the distance is so great between towns and the cost of transportation is so great?"

"No sir. This is the first circus I ever was to. I have never saw a circus before."

"How did you like it?"

"O, tip-top. It was a good thing. I'd like to see it every day if I could. I laughed and drank lemonade till I've got my cloze all

130

pinned up with pins, and I'd as soon tell you, if you won't give it away, that my pants is tied on me with barbed fence wire."

"Probably that's what gives you that anxious and apprehensive look?"

"Yes, sir. If I look kind of doubtless about something, its because I'm afraid my pantaloons will fall off on the floor and I will have to borrow a roller towel to wear home."

"How did you like the animals?"

"I liked that part of the Great Moral Aggregation the best of all. I have not saw such a sight before. I could stand there and watch that there old scaly elephant stuff hay into his bosom with his long rubber nose for hours. I'd read a good deal first and last about the elephant, the king of beasts, but I had never yet saw one. Yesterday father told me there hadn't been much joy into my young life, and so he gave me a dollar and told me to go over to the circus and have a grand time. I tell you, I just turned myself loose and gave myself up to pleasure."

"What other animals seemed to please you?" I asked, seeing that he was getting a little freer to talk.

"Oh, I saw the blue-nosed baboon from Farther India, and the red-eyed sandhill crane from Maddygasker, I think it was, and the sacred Jack-rabbit from Scandihoovia, and the lop-eared layme from South America. Then there was the female acrobat with her hair tied up with red ribbon. It's funny about them acrobat wimmen. They get big pay, but they never buy cloze with their money. Now the idea of a woman that gets $2 or $3 a day, for all I know, coming out there before 2,000 total strangers, wearing a pair of Indian war clubs and a red ribbon in her hair. I tell you, pardner, them acrobat prima donnars are mighty stingy with their money, or else they're mighty economical with their cloze."

"Did you go into the side show?"

"No sir. I studied the oil paintings on the outside, but I didn't go in. I met a handsome looking man there near the side show, though, that seemed to take an interest in me. There was a lottery along with the show and he wanted me to go and throw for him."

"Capper, probably?"

"Perhaps, so. Anyhow, he gave me a dollar and told me to go and throw for him."

"Why didn't he throw for himself?"

"Oh, he said the lottery man knew him and wouldn't let him throw."

"Of course, same old story. He saw you were a greeney and got you to throw for him. He stood in with the game so that you drew a big prize for the capper, created a big excitement, and you and the crowd sailed in and lost all the money you had. I'll bet he was a man with a velvet coat, and a moustache dyed a dead black and waxed as sharp as a cambric needle."

"Yes, that's his description to a dot. I wonder if he really did do that a-purpose."

"Well, tell us about it. It does me good to hear a blamed fool tell how he lost his money. Don't you see that your awkward ways and general greenness struck the capper the first thing, and you not only threw away your own money, but two or three hundred other wappy-jawed pelicans saw you draw a big prize and thought it was yours, then they deposited what little they had and everything was lovely."

"Well, I'll tell you how it was, if it'll do any good and save other young men in the future. You see this capper, as you call him, gave me a $1 bill to throw for him, and I put it into my vest pocket so, along with the dollar bill my father gave me. I always carry my money in my right hand vest pocket. Well, I sailed up to the game, big as old Jumbo himself, and put a dollar into the game. As you say, I drawed a big prize, $20 and a silver cup. The man offered me $5 for the cup and I took it."

"Then it flashed over my mind that I might have got my dollar and the other feller's mixed, so I says to the proprietor, 'I will now invest a dollar for a gent who asked me to draw for him.'

"Thereupon I took out the other dollar, and I'll be eternally chastised if I didn't draw a brass locket worth about two bits a bushel."

I didn't say anything for a long time. Then I asked him how the capper acted when he got his brass locket.

"Well, he seemed pained and grieved about something, and he asked me if I hadn't time to go away into a quiet place where we could talk it over by ourselves; but he had a kind of a cruel, insincere look in his eye, and I said no, I believed I didn't care to, and that I was a poor conversationalist, anyhow; and so I came away, and left him looking at his brass locket and kicking holes in the ground and using profane language."

"Afterward I saw him talking to the proprietor of the lottery, and I feel, somehow, that they had lost confidence in me. I heard them speak of me in a jeering tone of voice, and one said as I passed by: 'There goes the meek-eyed rural convict now,' and he used a horrid oath at the same time."

"If it hadn't been for that one little quincidence, there would have been nothing to mar the enjoyment of the occasion."

From *Remarks By Bill Nye.*

One Kind of Fool

A young man, with a plated watch-chain that would do to tie up a sacred elephant, came into Denver the other day from the East, on the Julesburg Short line, and told the hotel clerk that he had just returned from Europe, and was on his way across the continent with the intention of publishing a book of international information. He handed an oilcloth grip across the counter, registered in a bold, bad way and with a flourish that scattered the ink all over the clerk's white shirt front.

He was assigned to a quiet room on the fifth floor, that had been damaged by water a few weeks before by the fire department. After an hour or two spent in riding up and down the elevator and ringing for things that didn't cost anything, he oiled his hair and strolled into the diningroom with a severe air and sat down opposite a big cattle man, who never oiled his hair or stuck his nose into other people's business.

The European traveler entered into conversation with the cattle man. He told him all about Paris and the continent, meanwhile polishing his hands on the tablecloth and eating everything within reach. While he ate another man's dessert, he chatted on gaily about Cologne and pitied the cattle man who had to stay out on the bleak plains and watch the cows, while others paddled around Venice and acquired information in a foreign land.

At first the cattle man showed some interest in Europe, but after a while he grew quiet and didn't seem to enjoy it. Later on the European tourist, with soiled cuffs and auburn mane, ordered the waiters around in a majestic way to impress people with his greatness, tipped over the vinegar cruet into the salt and ate a slice of boiled egg out of another man's salad.

134

Casually a tall Kansas man strolled in and asked the European tourist what he was doing in Denver. The cattle man, who by the way, has been abroad five or six times and is as much at home in Paris as he is in Omaha, investigated the matter, and learned that the fresh French tourist had been herding hens on a chicken ranch in Kansas for six years, and had never seen blue water. He then took a few personal friends to the dining room door, and they watched the alleged traveler. He had just taken a long, refreshing drink from the finger bowl of his neighbor on the left and was at the moment trying to scoop up a lump of sugar with the wrong end of the tongs.

There are a good many fools who drift around through the world and dodge the authorities, but the most disastrous ass that I know is the man who goes west with two dollars and forty cents in his pocket, without brains enough to soil the most delicate cambric handkerchief, and tries to play himself for a savant with so much knowledge that he has to shed information all the time to keep his abnormal knowledge from hurting him.

From *Remarks By Bill Nye.*

Picnic Incidents

Camping out in summer for several weeks is a good thing generally. Freedom from social restraint and suspenders is a great luxury for a time, and nothing purifies the blood quicker, or makes a side of bacon taste more like snipe on toast, than the crisp ozone that floats through the hills and forests where man can monkey o'er the green grass without violating a city ordinance.

The picnic is an aggravation. It has just enough of civilization to be a nuisance, and not enough barbarism to make life seem a luxury. If our aim be to lean up against a tree all day in a short seersucker coat and ditto pantaloons that segregated while we were festooning the hammock, the picnic is the thing. If we desire to go home at night with a jelly symphony on each knee and a thousand-legged worm in each ear, we may look upon the picnic as a success.

But to those who wish to forget the past and live only in the booming present, to get careless of gain and breathe brand-new air that has never been used, to appease an irritated liver, or straighten out a torpid lung, let me say, pick out a high, dry clime, where there are trout enough to give you an excuse for going there, take what is absolutely necessary and no more, and then stay there long enough to have some fun.

If we picnic, we wear ourselves out trying to have a good time, so that we can tell about it when we get back, but we do not actually get acquainted with each other before we have to quit and return.

To camp, is to change the whole programme of life, and to stop long enough in the never-ending conflict for dollars and distinction, to get a full breath and look over the field. Still, it is not always smooth sailing. To camp, is sometimes to show the material

Charcoal Brown's Reproaches by J. H. Smith

of which we are made. The dude at home is the dude in camp, and wherever he goes he demonstrates that he was made for naught. I do not know what a camping party would do with a dude unless they used him to bait a bear trap with, and even then it would be taking a mean advantage of the bear. The bear certainly has some rights which we are bound in all decency to respect.

James Milton Sherrod said he had a peculiar experience once while he was in camp on the Poudre in Colorado.

"We went over from Larmy," said he, "in July, eight years ago —four of us. There was me and Charcoal Brown, and old Joe and young Joe Connoy. We had just got comfortably down on the Lower Fork, out of the reach of everybody and sixty miles from a doctor, when Charcoal Brown got sick. Wa'al, we had a big time of it. You can imagine yourself somethin' about it. Long in the night Brown began to groan and whoop and holler, and I made a diagnosis of him. He didn't have much sand anyhow. He was tryin' to git a pension from the government on the grounds of desertion and failure to provide, and some such a blame thing or another, so I didn't feel much sympathy fur him. But when I lit the gas and examined him, I found that he had a large fever on hand, and there we was without a doggon thing in the house but a jug of emigrant whiskey and a paper of condition powders fur the mule. I was a good deal rattled at first to know what the dickens to do fur him. The whiskey wouldn't do him any good, and besides, if he was goin' to have a long spell of sickness we needed it for the watchers.

"Wa'al, it was rough. I'd think of a thousand things that was good fur fevers, and then I'd remember that we hadn't got 'em. Finally old Joe says to me, 'James, why don't ye soak his feet?' says he. 'Soak nuthin',' says I; 'what would ye soak 'em in?' We had a long-handle frying-pan, and we could heat water in it, of course, but it was too shaller to do any good, anyhow; so we abandoned that synopsis right off. First I thought I'd try the condition powders in him, but I hated to go into a case and prescribe so recklessly. Finally I thought of a case of rheumatiz that I had up in Bitter Creek years ago, and how the boys filled their socks full of hot ashes and put 'em all over me till it started the persbyterian all over me and I got over it. So we begun to skirmish around the tent for socks, and I hope I may be tee-totally skun if there was a blame sock in the whole syndicate. Es fur me, I never wore 'em, but I did think young Joe would be fixed. He wasn't though. Said he didn't want to be considered proud and high strung, so he left his socks at home.

"Then we begun to look around and finally decided that Brown would die pretty soon if we didn't break up the fever, so we concluded to take all the ashes under the camp-fire, fill up his cloze, which was loose, tie his sleeves at the wrists, and his pants at the ankles, give him a dash of condition powders and a little whiskey to take the taste out of his mouth, and then see what ejosted nature would do.

"So we stood Brown up agin a tree and poured hot ashes down his back till he begun to fit his cloze pretty quick, and then we laid him down in the tent and covered him up with everything we had in our humble cot. Everything worked well till he begun to perspirate, and then there was music, and don't you forget it. That kind of soaked the ashes, don't you see, and made a lye that would take the peelin' off a telegraph pole.

"Charcoal Brown jest simply riz up and uttered a shrill whoop that jarred the geology of Colorado, and made my blood run cold. The goose flesh riz on old Joe Connoy till you could hang your hat on him anywhere. It was awful.

"Brown stood up on his feet, and threw things, and cussed us till we felt ashamed of ourselves. I've seen sickness a good deal in my time, but—I give it to you straight—I never seen an invalid stand up in the loneliness of the night, far from home and friends, with the concentrated lye oozin' out of the cracks of his boots, and reproach people the way Charcoal Brown did us.

"He got over it, of course, before Christmas, but he was a different man after that. I've been out campin' with him a good many times sence, but he never complained of feelin' indisposed. He seemed to be timid about tellin' us even if he was under the weather, and old Joe Connoy said mebbe Brown was afraid we would prescribe fur him or sumthin'."

From *Remarks By Bill Nye.*

The Duke of Rawhide by J. H. Smith

The Duke of Rawhide

"I believe I've got about the most instinct bulldog in the United States," said Cayote Van Gobb yesterday. "Other pups may show cuteness and cunning, you know, but my dog, the Duke of Rawhide Buttes, is not only generally smart, but he keeps up with the times. He's not only a talented cuss, but his genius is always fresh and original."

"What are some of his specialties, Van?" said I.

"Oh, there's a good many of 'em, fust and last. He never seems to be content with the achievements that please other dogs. You watch him and you'll see that his mind is active all the time. When he is still he's working up some scheme or another, that he will ripen and fructify later on.

"For three years I've had a watermelon patch and run it with more or less success, I reckon. The Duke has tended to 'em after they got ripe, and I was going to say that it kept his hands pretty busy to do it, but, to be more accurate, I should say that it kept his mouth full. Hardly a night after the melons got ripe and in the dark of the moon, but the Duke would sample a cowboy or a sheepherder from the lower Poudre. Watermelons were generally worth ten cents a pound along the Union Pacific for the first two weeks, and a fifty-pounder was worth $5. That made it an object to keep your melons, for in a good year you could grow enough on ten acres to pay off the national debt.

"Well, to return to my subject. Duke would sleep days during the season and gather fragments of the rear breadths of Western pantaloons at night. One morning Duke had a piece of fancy cassimere in his teeth that I tried to pry out and preserve, so that I could identify the owner, perhaps, but he wouldn't give it up. I coaxed him and lammed him across the face and eyes with an old board, but he wouldn't give it to me. Then I watched him. I've been watchin' him ever since. He took all these fragments of goods I found, over into the garret above the carriage shed.

"Yesterday I went in there and took a lantern with me. There on the floor the Duke of Rawhide had arranged all the samples of Rocky Mountain pantaloons with a good deal of taste, and I don't suppose you'd believe it, but that blamed pup is collecting all these little scraps to make himself a crazy quilt.

"You can talk about instinct in animals, but, so far as the Duke of Rawhide Buttes is concerned, it seems to me more like all-wool genius a yard wide."

From *Remarks By Bill Nye*.

A Resign

Postoffice Divan, Laramie City, W.T.
Oct. 1, 1883.

TO THE PRESIDENT OF THE UNITED STATES:

Sir.—I beg leave at this time to officially tender my resignation as postmaster at this place, and in due form to deliver the great seal and the key to the front door of the office. The safe combination is set on the numbers 33, 66 and 99, though I do not remember at this moment which comes first, or how many times you revolve the knob, or which direction you should turn it at first in order to make it operate.

There is some mining stock in my private drawer in the safe, which I have not yet removed. This stock you may have, if you desire it. It is a luxury, but you may have it. I have decided to keep a horse instead of this mining stock. The horse may not be so pretty, but it will cost less to keep him.

You will find the postal cards that have not been used under the distributing table, and the coal down in the cellar. If the stove draws too hard, close the damper in the pipe and shut the general delivery window.

Looking over my stormy and eventful administration as postmaster here, I find abundant cause for thanksgiving. At the time I entered upon the duties of my office the department was not yet on a paying basis. It was not even self-sustaining. Since that time, with the active co-operation of the chief executive and the heads of the department, I have been able to make our postal system a paying one, and on top of that I am now able to reduce the tariff on average-sized letters from three cents to two. I might add that this is rather too too, but I will not say anything that might seem

141

undignified in an official resignation which is to become a matter of history.

Through all the vicissitudes of a tempestuous term of office I have safely passed. I am able to turn over the office to-day in a highly improved condition, and to present a purified and renovated institution to my successor.

Acting under the advice of Gen. Hatton, a year ago, I removed the feather bed with which my predecessor, Deacon Hayford, had bolstered up his administration by stuffing the window, and substituted glass. Finding nothing in the book of instructions to postmasters which made the feather bed a part of my official duties, I filed it away in an obscure place and burned it in effigy, also in the gloaming. This act maddened my predecessor to such a degree, that he then and there became a candidate for justice of the peace on the Democratic ticket. The Democratic party was able, however, with what aid it secured from the Republicans, to plow the old man under to a great degree.

It was not long after I had taken my official oath before an era of unexampled prosperity opened for the American people. The price of beef rose to a remarkable altitude, and other vegetables commanded a good figure and a ready market. We then began to make active preparations for the introduction of the strawberry-roan two-cent stamps and the black-and-tan postal note. One reform has crowded upon the heels of another, until the country is to-day upon the foam-crested wave of permanent prosperity.

Mr. President, I cannot close this letter without thanking yourself and the heads of departments at Washington for your active, cheery and prompt co-operation in these matters. You can do as you see fit, of course, about incorporating this idea into your Thanksgiving proclamation, but rest assured it would not be ill-timed or inopportune. It is not alone a credit to myself. It reflects credit upon the administration also.

I need not say that I herewith transmit my resignation with great sorrow and genuine regret. We have toiled on together month after month, asking for no reward except the innate consciousness of rectitude and the salary as fixed by law. Now we are to separate. Here the roads seem to fork, as it were, and you and I, and the cabinet, must leave each other at this point.

You will find the key under the door-mat, and you had better turn the cat out at night when you close the office. If she does not go readily, you can make it clearer to her mind by throwing the canceling stamp at her.

If Deacon Hayford does not pay up his box-rent, you might as well put his mail in the general delivery, and when Bob Head gets drunk and insists on a letter from one of his wives every day in the week, you can salute him through the box delivery with an old Queen Anne tomahawk, which you will find near the Etruscan water-pail. This will not in any manner surprise either of these parties.

Tears are unavailing. I once more become a private citizen, clothed only with the right to read such postal cards as may be addressed to me personally, and to curse the inefficiency of the postoffice department. I believe the voting class to be divided into two parties, viz: Those who are in the postal service, and those who are mad because they cannot receive a registered letter every fifteen minutes of each day, including Sunday.

Mr. President, as an official of this Government I now retire. My term of office would not expire until 1886. I must, therefore, beg pardon for my eccentricity in resigning. It will be best, perhaps, to keep the heart-breaking news from the ears of European powers until the dangers of a financial panic are fully past. Then hurl it broadcast with a sickening thud.

From *Remarks By Bill Nye.*

Squaw Jim

"Jim, you long-haired, backslidden Caucasian nomad, why don't you say somethin? Brace up and tell us your experience. Were you kidnapped when you were a kid and run off into the wild wickyup of the forest, or how was it that you came to leave the Yankee reservation and eat the raw dog of the Sioux?"

We were all sitting around the roaring fat-pine fire at the foot of the canon, and above us the full moon was filling the bottom of the black notch in the mountains, where God began to engrave the gulch that grew wider and deeper till it reached the valley where we were.

Squaw Jim was tall, silent and grave. He was as dignified as the king of clubs, and as reticent as the private cemetery of a deaf and dumb asylum. He didn't move when Dutch Joe spoke to him, but he noticed the remark, and after awhile got up in the firelight, and later on the silent savage made the longest speech of his life.

"Boys, you call me Squaw Jim, and you call my girl a half breed. I have no other name than Squaw Jim with the pale faced dude and the dyspeptic sky pilot who tells me of his God. You call me Squaw Jim because I've married a squaw and insist on living with her. If I had married Mist-of-the-Waterfall, and had lived in my tepee with her summers, and wintered at St. Louis with a wife who belonged to a tall peaked church, and who wore her war paint, and her false scalp-lock, and her false heart into God's wigwam, I'd be all right probably. They would have laughed about it a little among the boys, but it would have been "wayno" in the big stone lodges at the white man's city.

"I loved a pale faced girl in Connecticut forty years ago. She said she did me, but she met with a change of heart and married a bare-back rider in a circus. Then she ran away with the sword

144

swallower of the side show, and finally broke her neck trying to walk the tight rope. The jury said if the rope had been as tight as she was it might have saved her life.

"Since then I've been where the sun and the air and the soil were free. It kind of soothed me to wear moccasins and throw my biled shirt into the Missouri. It took the fever of jealousy and disappointment out of my soul to sleep in the great bosom of the unhoused night. Soon I learned how to parley-vous in the Indian language, and to wear the clothes of the red man. I married the squaw girl who saved me from the mountain fever and my foes. She did not yearn for the equestrian of the white man's circus. She didn't know how to raise XxYxZ to the nth power, but she was a wife worthy of the President of the United States. She was way off the trail in matters of etiquette, but she didn't know what it was to envy and hate the pale faced squaw with the sealskin sacque and the torpid liver, and the high-priced throne of grace. She never sighed to go where they are filling up Connecticut's celestial exhibit with girls who get mysteriously murdered and the young men who did it go out lecturing. You see I keep posted.

"Boys, you kind of pity me, I reckon, and say Squaw Jim might have been in Congress if he'd stayed with his people and wore night shirts and pared his claws, but you needn't.

"My wife can't knock the tar out of a symphony on the piano, but she can mop the dew off the grass with a burglar, and knock out a dude's eyes at sixty yards rise.

"My wife is a little foggy on the winter style of salvation, and probably you'd stall her on how to drape a silk velvet overskirt so it wouldn't hang one-sided, but she has a crude idea of an every day, all wool General Superintendent of the Universe and Father of all-Humanity, whether they live under a horse blanket tepee or a Gothic mortgage. She might look out of place before the cross, with her chilblains, and her childlike confidence, among the Tom cat sealskin sacques of your camel's hair Christianity, but if the world was supplied with Christians like my wife, purgatory would make an assignment, and the Salvation Army would go home and hoe corn. Sabe?"

From *Remarks By Bill Nye.*

Man Overbored

"Speaking about prohibition," said Misery Brown one day, while we sat lying on the dump of the *Blue Tail Fly*, "I am prone to allow that the more you prohibit, the more you—all at once— discover that you have more or less failed to prohibit.

"Now, you can win a man over to your way of thinking, some- times, but you mustn't do it with the butt-end of a telegraph pole. You might convert him that way, perhaps, but the mental shock and phrenological concussion of the argument might be disastrous to the convert himself.

"A man once said to me that rum was the devil's drink, that Satan's home was filled with the odor of hot rum, that perdition was soaked with spiced rum and rum punch. 'You wot not,' said he, 'the ruin rum has rot. Why, Misery Brown,' said he, 'rum is my *bete noir*.' I said I didn't care what he used it for, he's always find it very warming to the system. I told him he could use it for a hot *bete noir*, or a *blanc mange*, or any of those fancy drinks; I didn't care.

"But the worst time I ever had grappling with the great enemy, I reckon, was in the later years of the war, when I pretty near squashed the rebellion. Grim-visaged war had worn me down pretty well. I played the big tuba in the regimental band, and I began to sigh for peace.

"We had been on the march all summer, it seemed to me. We'd travel through dust ankle-deep all day that was just like ashes, and halt in the red-hot sun five minutes to make coffee. We'd make our coffee in five minutes and sometimes we'd make it in the middle of the road; but that's neither here nor there.

"We finally found out that we would make a stand in a certain town, and that the Q.M. had two barrels of old and reliable whisky in store. We also found out that we couldn't get any for medical purposes nor anything else. All we could do was to suffer on and wait till the war closed. I didn't feel like postponing the thing myself, so I began to investigate. The great foe of humanity was stored in a tobacco-house, and the Q.M. slept three nights between the barrels. The chances for a debauch looked peaked and slim in the extreme. However, there was a basement below, and I got in there one night with a half-inch auger, and two washtubs. Later on there was a sound of revelry by night. There was considerable 'on with the dance, let joy be unconfined.'

"The next day there was a spongy appearance to the top of the head, which seemed to be confined to our regiment, as a result of the sudden giving way, as it were, of prohibitory restrictions. It was a very disagreeable day, I remember. All nature seemed clothed in gloom, and R. E. Morse, P.D.Q., seemed to be in charge of the proceedings. Redeyed Regret was everywhere.

"We then proceeded to yearn for the other barrel of woe, that we might pile up some more regret, and have enough misery to last us through the balance of the campaign. We acted on this suggestion, and, with a firm resolve and the same half-inch auger, we stole once more into the basement of the tobacco-house.

"I bored nineteen consecutive holes in the atmosphere, and then an intimate friend of mine bored twenty-seven distinct holes in the floor, only to bore through the bosom of the night. Eleven of us spent the most of the night boring into the floor, and at three o'clock A.M. it looked like a hammock, it was so full of holes. The Quartermaster slept on through all of it. He slept in a very audible tone of voice, and every now and then we could hear him slumbering on.

"At last we decided that he was sleeping middling close to that barrel, so we began to bore closer to the snore. It was my turn to bore, I remember, and I took the auger with a heavy heart. I bored through the floor, and for the first time bored into something besides oxygen. It was the quartermaster. A wild yell echoed through the southern confederacy, and I pulled out my auger. It had on the point a strawberry mark, and a fragment of one of those old-fashioned woven wire gray shirts, such as quartermasters used to wear.

"I remember that we then left the tobacco-house. In the hurry we forgot two wash-tubs, a half-inch auger, and 980,361 new half-inch auger holes that had never been used."

From *Remarks By Bill Nye*.

The Cow-Boy

So much amusing talk is being made recently anent the blood-bedraggled cow-boy of the wild West, that I rise as one man to say a few things, not in a dictatorial style, but regarding this so-called or so esteemed dry land pirate who, mounted on a little cow-pony and under the black flag, sails out across the green surge of the plains to scatter the rocky shores of Time with the bones of his fellow-man.

A great many people wonder where the cow-boy, with his abnormal thirst for blood, originated. Where did this young Jesse James, with his gory record and his dauntless eye, come from? Was he born in a buffalo wallow at the foot of some rock-ribbed mountain, or did he first breathe the thin air along the brink of an alkali pond, where the horned toad and the centipede sang him to sleep, and the tarantula tickled him under the chin with its hairy legs?

Careful research and cold, hard statistics show that the cow-boy, as a general thing, was born in an unostentatious manner on the farm. I hate to sit down on a beautiful romance and squash the breath out of a romantic dream; but the cow-boy who gets too much moist damnation in his system, and rides on a gallop up and down Main street shooting out the lights of the beautiful billiard palaces, would be just as unhappy if a mouse ran up his pantaloon-leg as you would, gentle reader. He is generally a youth who thinks he will not earn his twenty-five dollars per month if he does not yell, and whoop, and shoot, and scare little girls into St. Vitus's dance. I've known more cow-boys to injure themselves with their own revolvers than to injure anyone else. This is evidently because they are more familiar with the hoe than they are with the Smith & Wesson.

One night, while I had rooms in the business part of a Territorial city in the Rocky Mountain cattle country, I was awakened at about one o'clock A.M. by the most blood-curdling cry of "Murder" I ever heard. It was murder with a big "M." Across the street, in the bright light of a restaurant, a dozen cow-boys with broad sombreros and flashing silver braid, huge leather chaperajas, Mexican spurs and orange silk neckties, and with flashing revolvers, were standing. It seemed that a big, red-faced Captain Kidd of the band, with his skin full of valley tan, had marched into an ice-cream resort with a self-cocker in his hand, and ordered the vanilla coolness for the gang. There being a dozen young folks at the place, mostly male and female, from a neighboring hop, indulging in cream, the proprietor, a meek Norwegian with thin white hair, deemed it rude and outre to do so. He said something to that effect whereat the other eleven men of alcoholic courage let off a yell that froze the cream into a solid glacier, and shook two kerosene lamps out of their sockets in the chandeliers.

Thereupon the little Y.M.C.A. Norwegian said:

"Gentlemans, I kain't neffer like dot squealinks and dot kaind of a tings, and you fellers mit dot ledder pantses on and dot funny glose and such a tings like dot, better keep kained of quiet, or I shall call up the policemen mit my delephone."

Then they laughed at him, and cried yet again with a loud voice.

This annoyed the ice-cream agriculturist, and he took the old axe-handle that he used to jam the ice down around the freezer with, and peeled a large area of scalp off the leader's dome of thought, and it hung down over his eyes, so that he could not see to shoot with any degree of accuracy.

After he had yelled "Murder!" three or four times, he fell under an ice-cream table, and the mild-eyed Scandinavian broke a silver-plated castor over the organ of self-esteem, and poured red pepper, and salt, and vinegar, and Halford sauce and other relishes, on the place where the scalp was loose.

This revived the brave but murderous cow-gentleman, and he begged that he might be allowed to go away.

The gentle Y.M.C.A. superintendent of the ten-stamp ice-cream freezers then took the revolvers away from the bold buccaneer, and kicked him out through a show-case, and saluted him with a bouquet of July oysters that suffered severely from malaria.

All cow-boys are not sanguinary; but out of twenty you will generally find one who is brave when he has his revolvers with him; but when he forgot and left his shooters at home on the piano, the most tropical violet-eyed dude can climb him with the butt-end of a sunflower, and beat his brains out and spatter them all over that school district.

In the wild, unfettered West, beware of the man who never carries arms, never gets drunk and always minds his own business. He don't go around shooting out the gas, or intimidating a kindergarten school; but when a brave frontiersman, with a revolver in each boot and a bowie down the back of his neck, insults a modest young lady, and needs to be thrown through a plate-glass window and then walked over by the populace, call on the silent man who dares to wear a clean shirt and human clothes.

From *Remarks By Bill Nye.*

Early Day Justice

Those were troublesome times, indeed. All wool justice in the courts was impossible. The vigilance committee, or Salvation Army as it called itself, didn't make much fuss about it, but we all knew that the best citizens belonged to it and were in good standing.

It was in those days when young Stewart was short-handed for a sheepherder and had to take up with a sullen, hairy vagrant, called by the other boys "Esau." Esau hadn't been on the ranch a week before he made trouble with the proprietor and got the red-hot blessing from Stewart he deserved.

Then Esau got madder and sulked away down the valley among the little sage brush hummocks and white alkali waste land to nurse his wrath. When Stewart drove into the corral at night, from town, Esau raised up from behind an old sheep dip tank, and without a word except what may have growled around in his black heart, he raised a leveled Spencer and shot his young employer dead.

That was the tragedy of the week only. Others had occurred before and others would probably occur again. It was getting too prevalent for comfort. So, as soon as a quick cayuse and a boy could get down into town, the news spread and the authorities began in the routine manner to set the old legal mill to running. Someone had to go down to The Tivoli and find the prosecuting attorney, then a messenger had to go to The Alhambra for the justice of the peace. The prosecuting attorney was "full" and the judge had just drawn one card to complete a straight flush, and had succeeded.

In the meantime the Salvation Army was fully half way to Clugston's ranch. They had started out, as they said, "to see that

152

Esau didn't get away." They were going out there to see that Esau was brought into town. What happened after they got there I only know from hearsay, for I was not a member of the Salvation Army at that time. But I got it from one of those present, that they found Esau down in the sage brush down on the bottoms that lie between the abrupt corner of Sheep Mountain and the Little Laramie River. They captured him, but he died soon after, as it was told to me, from the effects of opium taken with suicidal intent. I remember seeing Esau the next morning and I thought there were signs of ropium, as there was a purple streak around the neck of the deceased, together with other external phenomena not peculiar to opium.

But the great difficulty with the Salvation Army was that it didn't want to bring Esau into town. A long, cold night ride with a person in Esau's condition was disagreeable. Twenty miles of lonely road with a deceased murderer in the bottom of the wagon is depressing. Those of my readers who have tried it will agree with me that it is not calculated to promote hilarity. So the Salvation Army stopped at Whatley's ranch to get warm, hoping that someone would steal the remains and elope with them. They stayed some time and managed to "give away" the fact that there was a reward of $5,000 out for Esau, dead or alive. The Salvation Army even went so far as to betray a great deal of hilarity over the easy way it had nailed the reward, or would as soon as said remains were delivered up and identified.

Mr. Whatley thought that the Salvation Army was having a kind of walkaway, so he slipped out at the back door of the ranch, put Esau into his wagon and drove away to town. Remember, this is the way it was told to me. Mr. Whatley hadn't gone more than half a mile when he heard the wild and disappointed yells of the Salvation Army. He put the buckskin on the backs of his horses without mercy, driven on by the enraged shouts and yells of his infuriated pursuers. He reached town about midnight, and his pursuers disappeared. But what was he to do with Esau?

He drove around all over town, trying to find the official who sighed for the deceased. Mr. Whatley went from house to house like a vegetable man, seeking sadly for the party who would give him a $5,000 check for Esau. Nothing could be more depressing than to wake up one man after another out of a sound sleep and invite him to come out to the buggy and identify the remains. One man went out and looked at him. He said he didn't know how others felt about it, but he allowed that anybody who would pay $5,000 for such a remains as Esau's could not have very good taste.

Gradullay it crept thru Mr. Whatley's wool that the Salvation Army had been working him, so he left Esau at the engine house and went home. On his ranch he nailed up a large board on which had been painted in antique characters with a paddle and tar the following stanzas: Vigilance Committees, Salvation Armies, Morgues, or young physicians who may have deceased people on their hands, are requested to refrain from conferring them on to the undersigned. People who contemplate shuffling off their own or other people's mortal coils, will please not do so on these grounds. The Salvation Army of the Rocky Mts is especially warned to keep off the grass!
James Whatley.

From *Remarks By Bill Nye*.

My Dog

I have owned quite a number of dogs in my life, but they are all dead now. Last evening I visited my dog cemetery—just between the gloaming and the shank of the evening. On the biscuit-box cover that stands at the head of a little mound fringed with golden rod and pickle bottles, the idler may still read these lines, etched in red chalk by a trembling hand:

> Little Kosciusko,
> ——NOT DEAD——
> But Jerked Hence
> By Request
> S.Y.L.
> (see you later.) ⁻

I do not know why he was called Kosciusko. I do not care. I only know that his little grave stands out there while the gloaming gloams and the soughing winds are soughing.

Do you ask why I am alone here and dogless in this weary world?

I will tell you, anyhow. It will not take long, and it may do me good:

Kosciusko came to me one night in winter, with no baggage and unidentified. When I opened the door he came in as though he had left something in there by mistake and had returned for it.

He stayed with us two years as a watch-dog. In a desultory way, he was a good watch-dog. If he had watched other people with the same unrelenting scrutiny with which he watched me, I might have felt his death more keenly than I do now.

The second year that little Kosciusko was with us, I shaved off a full beard one day while down town, put on a clean collar and otherwise disguised myself, intending to surprise my wife.

155

Kosciusko sat on the front porch when I returned. He looked at me as the cashier of a bank does when a newspaper man goes in to get a suspiciously large check cashed. He did not know me. I said, "Kosciusko, have you forgotten your master's voice?"

He smiled sarcastically, showing his glorious wealth of mouth, but still sat there as though he had stuck his tail into the doorsteps and couldn't get it out.

So I waived the formality of going in at the front door, and went around to the portcullis, on the off side of the house, but Kosciusko was there when I arrived. The cook, seeing a stranger lurking around the manor house, encouraged Kosciusko to come and gorge himself with a part of my leg, which he did. Acting on this hint I went to the barn. I do not know why I went to the barn but somehow there was nothing in the house that I wanted. When a man wants to be by himself, there is no place like a good, quiet barn for thought. So I went into the barn, about three feet prior to Kosciusko.

Noticing the stairway, I ascended it in an aimless kind of way, about four steps at a time. What happened when we got into the haymow I do not now recall, only that Kosciusko and I frolicked around there in the hay for some time. Occasionally I would be on top, and then he would have all the delegates, until finally I got hold of a pitchfork, and freedom shrieked when Kosciusko fell. I wrapped myself up in an old horse-net and went into the house. Some of my clothes were afterward found in the hay, and the doctor pried a part of my person out of Kosciusko's jaws, but not enough to do me any good.

I have owned, in all, eleven dogs, and they all died violent deaths, and went out of the world totally unprepared to die.

From *Remarks By Bill Nye.*

Rev. Mr. Hallelujah's Hoss

There are a good many difficult things to ride, I find, beside the bicycle and the bucking Mexican plug. Those who have tried to mount and successfully ride a wheelbarrow in the darkness of the stilly night will agree with me.

You come on a wheelbarrow suddenly when it is in a brown study, and you undertake to straddle it, so to speak, and all at once you find the wheelbarrow on top. I may say, I think safely that the wheelbarrow is, as a rule, phlegmatic and cool; but when a total stranger startles it, it spreads desolation and destruction on every hand.

This is also true of the perambulator, or baby-carriage. I undertook to evade a child's phaeton, three years ago last spring, as it stood in the entrance to a hall in Main Street. The child was not injured, because it was not in the carriage at the time; but I was not so fortunate. I pulled pieces of perambulator out of myself for two weeks with the hand that was not disabled.

How a sedentary man could fall through a child's carriage in such a manner as to stab himself with the awning and knock every spoke out of three wheels, is still a mystery to me, but I did it. I can show you the doctor's bill now.

The other day, however, I discovered a new style of riding animal. The Rev. Mr. Hallelujah was at the depot when I arrived, and was evidently waiting for the same Chicago train that I was in search of. Rev. Mr. Hallelujah had put his valise down near an ordinary baggage-truck which leaned up against the wall of the station building.

He strolled along the platform a few moments, communing with himself and agitating his mind over the subject of Divine Retribution, and then he went up and leaned against the truck. Finally, he somehow got his arms under the handles of the truck as it stood up between his back and the wall. He still continued to think of the plan of Divine Retribution, and you could have seen his lips move if you had been there.

Pretty soon some young ladies came along, rosy in winter air, beautiful beyond compare, frosty crystals in their hair; smiled they on the preacher there.

He returned the smile and bowed low. As he did so, as near as I can figure it out, he stepped back on the iron edge of the truck that the baggage-man generally jabs under the rim of an iron-bound sample-trunk when he goes to load it. Anyhow, Mr. Hallelujah's feet flew toward next spring. The truck started across the platform with him and spilled him over the edge on the track ten feet below. So rapid was the movement that the eye with difficulty followed his evolutions. His valise was carried onward by the same wild avalanche, and "busted" open before it struck the track below.

I was surprised to see some of the articles that shot forth into the broad light of day. Among the rest there was a bran fired new set of ready-made teeth, to be used in case of accident. Up to that moment I didn't know that Mr. Hallelujah used the common tooth of commerce. These teeth slipped out of the valise with a Sabbath smile and vulcanized rubber gums.

In striking the iron track below, the every-day set which the Rev. Mr. Hallelujah had in use became loosened, and smiled across the road-bed and right of way at the bran fired new array of incisors, cuspids, bicuspids and molars that flew out of the valise. Mr. Hallelujah got up and tried to look merry, but he could not smile without his teeth. The back seams of his Newmarket coat were more successful, however.

Mr. Hallelujah's wardrobe and a small boy were the only objects that dared to smile.

From *Remarks By Bill Nye.*

A Father's Letter

My dear Son.—Your letter of last week reached us yesterday, and I enclose $13, which is all I have by me at the present time. I may sell the other shote next week and make up the balance of what you wanted. I will probably have to wear the old buffalo overcoat to meetings again this winter, but that don't matter so long as you are getting an education.

I hope you will get your education as cheap as you can, for it cramps your mother and me like Sam Hill to put up the money. Mind you, I don't complain. I knew education come high, but I didn't know the clothes cost so like sixty.

I want you to be so that you can go anywhere and spell the hardest word. I want you to be able to go among the Romans or the Medes and Persians and talk to any of them in their own native tongue.

I never had any advantages when I was a boy, but your mother and I decided that we would sock you full of knowledge, if your liver held out, regardless of expense. We calculate to do it, only we want you to go as slow on swallow-tail coats as possible till we can sell our hay.

Now, regarding that boat-paddling suit, and that baseball suit, and that bathing suit, and that roller-rinktum suit, and that lawn-tennis suit, mind, I don't care about the expense, because you say a young man can't really educate himself thoroughly without them, but I wish you'd send home what you get through with this fall and I'll wear them through the winter under my other clothes. We have a good deal severer winters here than we used to, or else I'm failing in bodily health. Last winter I tried to go through without underclothes, the way I did when I was a boy, but a Manitoba wave came down our way and picked me out of a crowd with its eyes shet.

In your last letter you alluded to getting injured in a little "hazing scuffle with a pelican from the rural districts." I don't want any harm to come to you, my son, but if I went from the rural districts, and another young gosling from the rural districts undertook to haze me, I would swat him across the back of the neck with a fence board, and then I would meander across the pit of his stomach and put a blue forget-me-not under his eye.

Your father ain't much on Grecian mythology and how to get the square root of a barrel of pork, but he wouldn't allow any educational institutions to haze him with impunity. Perhaps you remember once when you tried to haze your father a little, just to kill time, and how long it took you to recover. Anybody that goes at it right can have a good deal of fun with your father, but those who have sought to monkey with him, just to break up the monotony of life, have most always succeeded in finding what they sought.

I ain't much of a pensman, so you will have to excuse this letter. We are all quite well, except old Fan, who has a galded shoulder, and hope this will find you enjoying the same great blessing.

Your Father

From *Remarks By Bill Nye.*

Taxidermy

This name is from two Greek words which signify "arrangement" and "skin," so that the ancient Greeks, no doubt, regarded taxidermy as the original skin-game of that period. Taxidermy did not flourish in America prior to the year 1828. At that time an Englishman named Scudder established a museum and general repository for upholstered beasts.

Since then the art has advanced quite rapidly. To properly taxiderm, requires a fine taste and a close study of the subject itself in life, akin to the requirements necessary in order to succeed as a sculptor. I have seen taxidermed animals that would fool anybody. I recall, at this time especially, a mountain lion, stuffed after death by a party who had not made this matter a subject of close study. The lion was represented in a crouching attitude, with open jaws and red gums. As time passed on and year succeeded year, this lion continued to crouch. His tail became less rampant and drooped like a hired man on a hot day. His gums became less fiery red and his reddish skin hung over his bones in a loose and distraught manner, like an old buffalo robe thrown over the knees of a vinegary old maid. Spiders spun their webs across his dull, white fangs. Mice made their nests in his abdominal cavity. His glass eye became hoplessly strabismussed, and the moths left him bald-headed on the stomach. He was a sad commentary on the extremely transitory nature of all things terrestrial and the hollowness of the stuffed beast.

I had a stuffed bird for a long time, which showed the cunning of the stuffer to a great degree. It afforded me a great deal of unalloyed pleasure, because I like to get old hunters to look at it and tell me what kind of a bird it was. They did not generally agree. A bitter and acrimonious fight grew out of a discussion in relation to

161

this bird. A man from Vinegar Hill named Lyons and a party called Soiled Murphy (since deceased), were in my office one morning—Mr. Lyons as a witness, and Mr. Murphy in his great specialty as a drunk and disorderly. We had just disposed of the case, and had just stepped down from the bench, intending to take off the judicial ermine and put some more coal in the stove, when the attention of Soiled Murphy was attracted to the bird. We allowed that it was a common "hell-diver with an abnormal head," while Lyons claimed that it was a kingfisher.

The bird had a duck's body, the head of a common eagle and the feet of a sage hen. These parts had been adjusted with great care and the tail loaded with lead somehow, so that the powerful head would not tip the bird up behind. With this *rara avis*, to use a foreign term, I loved to amuse and instruct old hunters, who had been hunting all their lives for a free drink, and hear them tell how they had killed hundreds of these birds over on the Poudre in an early day, or over near Elk Mountain when the country was new.

So Lyons claimed that he had killed millions of these fowls, and Soiled Murphy, who was known as the tomato can and beer-remnant savant of that country, said that before the Union Pacific Railroad got into that section, these birds swarmed around Hutton's lakes and lived on horned toads.

The feeling got more and more partisan till Mr. Lyons made a pass at Soiled Murphy with a large red cuspidor that had been presented to me by Valentine Baker, a dealer in abandoned furniture and mines. Mr. Murphy then welted Lyons over the head with the judicial scales. He then adroitly caught a lump of bituminous coal with his countenance and fell to the floor with a low cry of pain.

I called in an outside party as a witness, and in the afternoon both men were convicted of assault and battery. Soiled Murphy asked for a change of venue on the ground that I was prejudiced. I told him that I did not allow anything whatever to prejudice me, and went on with the case.

This great taxidermic masterpiece led to other assaults afterward, all of which proved remunerative in a small way. My successor claimed that the bird was a part of the perquisites of the office, and so I had to turn it over with the docket.

I also had a stuffed weasel from Cummins City that attracted a great deal of attention, both in this country and in Europe. It looked some like a weasel and some like an equestrian sausage with hair on it.

From *Remarks By Bill Nye.*

Petticoats at the Polls

There have been many reasons given, first and last, why women should not vote, but I desire to say, in the full light of a ripe experience, that some of them are fallacious. I refer more particularly to the argument that it will degrade women to go to the polls and vote like a little man. While I am not and have never been a howler for female suffrage, I must admit that it is much more of a success than prohibition and speculative science.

My wife voted eight years with my full knowledge and consent, and today I cannot see but that she is as docile and as tractable as when she won my trusting heart.

Now those who know me best will admit that I am not a ladies' man, and, therefore, what I may say here is not said to secure favor and grateful smiles. I am not attractive and I am not in politics. I believe that I am homelier this winter than usual. There are reasons why I believe that what I may say on this subject will be sincere and not sensational or selfish.

It has been urged that good women do not generally exercise the right of suffrage, when they have the opportunity, and that only those whose social record has been tarnished a good deal go to the polls. This is not true.

It is the truth that a good full vote always shows a list of the best women and the wives of the best men. A bright day makes a better showing of lady voters than a bad one, and the weather makes a more perceptible difference in the female vote than the male, but when things are exciting and the battle is red-hot, and the tocsin of war sounds anon, the wife and mother puts on her armor and her sealskin sacque and knocks things cross-eyed.

It is generally supposed that the female voter is a pantaloonatic, a half horse, half alligator kind of woman, who looks like Dr.

Mary Walker and has the appearance of one who has risen hastily in the night at the alarm of fire and dressed herself partially in her own garments and partially in her husband's. This is a popular error. In Wyoming, where female suffrage has raged for years, you meet quiet, courteous and gallant gentlemen, and fair, quiet, sensible women at the polls, where there isn't a loud or profane word, and where it is an infinitely more proper place to send a young lady unescorted than to the postoffice in any city in the Union. You can readily see why this is so. The men about the polls are always candidates and their friends. That is the reason that neither party can afford to show the slightest rudeness toward a voter. The man who on Wednesday would tell her to go and soak her head, perhaps, would stand bareheaded to let her pass on Tuesday. While she holds a smashed ballot shoved under the palm of her gray kid glove she may walk over the candidate's prostrate form with impunity and her overshoes if she chooses to.

Weeks and months before election in Wyoming, the party with the longest purse subsidizes the most livery stables and carriages. Then, on the eventful day, every conveyance available is decorated with a political placard and driven by a polite young man who is instructed to improve the time. Thus every woman in Wyoming has a chance to ride once a year, at least. Lately, however, many prefer to walk to the polls, and they go in pairs, trios and quartettes, voting their little sentiments and calmly returning to their cookies and crazy quilts as though politics didn't jar their mental poise a minute.

It is possible, and even probable, that a man and his wife may disagree on politics as they might on religion. The husband may believe in Andrew Jackson and a relentless hell, while his wife may be a stalwart and rather liberal on the question of eternal punishment. If the husband manages his wife as he would a clotheswringer, and turns her through life by a crank, he will, no doubt, work her politically; but if she has her own ideas about things, she will naturally act upon them, while the man who is henpecked in other matters till he can't see out of his eyes, will be henpecked, no doubt, in the matter of national and local politics.

These are a few facts about the actual workings of female suffrage, and I do not tackle the great question of the ultimate results upon the political machinery if woman suffrage were to become general. I do not pretend to say as to that. I know a great deal, but I do not know that. There are millions of women, no doubt, who are better qualified to vote, and yet cannot, than millions of alleged men who do vote; but no one can tell now what the ultimate effect of a change might be.

So far as Wyoming is concerned, the Territory is prosperous and happy. I see, also, that a murderer was hung by process of law there the other day. That looks like the onward march of reform, whether female suffrage had anything to do with it or not. And they're going to hang another in March if the weather is favorable and executive clemency remains dormant, as I think it will.

All these things look hopeful. We can't tell what the Territory would have been without female suffrage, but when they begin to hang men by law instead of by moonlight, the future begins to brighten up. When you have to get up in the night to hang a man every little while and don't get any per diem for it, you feel as though you were a good way from home.

From *Remarks By Bill Nye*.

The Opium Habit

I have always had a horror of opiates of all kinds. They are seductive and so still in their operations. They steal through the blood like a wolf on the trail, and they seize upon the heart at last with their white fange till it is still forever.

Up the Laramie there is a cluster of ranches at the base of the Medicine Bow, near the north end of Sheep Mountain, and in sight of the glittering, eternal frost of the snowy range. These ranches are the homes of the young men from Massachusetts, Pennsylvania and Ohio, and now there are several "younger sons" of Old England, with herds of horses, steers and sheep, worth millions of dollars. These young men are not of the kind of whom the metropolitan ass writes as saying "youbetcherlife," and calling everybody "pardner." They are many of them college graduates, who can brand a wild Maverick or furnish the easy gestures for a Strauss waltz.

They wear human clothes, talk in the United States language, and have a bank account. This spring they may be wearing chaparajos and swinging a quirt through the thin air, and in July they may be at Long Branch, or coloring a meerschaum pipe among the Alps.

Well, a young man whom we will call Curtis lived at one of these ranches years ago, and, though a quiet, mind-your-own-business fellow, who had absolutely no enemies among his companions, he had the misfortune to incur the wrath of a tramp sheep-herder, who waylaid Curtis one afternoon and shot him dead as he sat in his buggy. Curtis wasn't armed. He didn't dream of trouble till he drove home from town, and, as he passed through the gates of a corral, saw the hairy face of the herder, and at the same moment the flash of a Winchester rifle. That was all.

167

A rancher came into town and telegraphed to Curtis' father, and then a half dozen citizens went out to help capture the herder, who had fled to the sage brush of the foot-hills.

They didn't get back till toward daybreak, but they brought the herder with them. I saw him in the gray of the morning, lying in a coarse gray blanket, on the floor of the engine house. He was dead.

I asked as a reporter, how he came to his death, and they told me—opium! I said, did I understand you to say "ropium?" They said no, it was opium. The murderer had taken poison when he found that escape was impossible.

I was present at the inquest, so that I could report the case. There was very little testimony, but all the evidence seemed to point to the fact that life was extinct, and a verdict of death by his own hand was rendered.

It was the first opium work I had ever seen, and it aroused my curiosity. Death by opium, it seems, leaves a dark purple ring around the neck. I did not know this before. People who die by opium also tie their hands together before they die. This is one of the eccentricities of opium poisoning that I have never seen laid down in the books. I bequeath it to medical science. Whenever I run up against a new scientific discovery, I just hand it right over to the public without cost.

Ever since the above incident, I have been very apprehensive about people who seem to be likely to form the opium habit. It is one of the most deadly of narcotics, especially in a new country. High up in the pure mountain atmosphere, this man could not secure enough air to prolong life, and he expired. In a land where clear, crisp air and delightful scenery are abundant, he turned his back upon them both and passed away. Is it not sad to contemplate?

From *Remarks By Bill Nye.*

A Father's Advice to His Son

MY DEAR HENRY.—

Your pensive favor of the 20th inst., asking for more means with which to persecute your studies, and also a young man from Ohio, is at hand and carefully noted.

I would not be ashamed to have you show the foregoing sentence to your teacher, if it could be worked, in a quiet way, so as not to look egotistic on my part. I think myself that it is pretty fair for a man that never had any advantages.

But, Henry, why will you insist on fighting the young man from Ohio? It is not only rude and wrong, but you invariably get licked. There's where the enormity of the thing comes in.

It was this young man from Ohio, named Williams, that you hazed last year, or at least that's what I gether from a letter sent me by your warden. He maintains that you started in to mix Mr. Williams up with the campus in some way, and that in some way Mr. Williams resented it and got his fangs tangled up in the bridge of your nose.

You never wrote this to me or to your mother, but I know how busy you are with your studies, and I hope you won't ever neglect your books just to write to us.

Your warden or whoever he is, said that Mr. Williams also hung a hand-painted marine view over your eye and put an extra eyelid on one of your ears.

I wish that, if you get time, you would write us about it, because, if there's anything I can do for you in the arnica line, I would be pleased to do so.

The President also says that in the scuffle you and Mr. Williams swapped belts as follows, to-wit: That Williams snatched off the belt of your little Norfolk jacket, and then gave you one in the eye.

From this I gether that the old prez, as you faseshusly call him, is an youmorist. He is not a very good penman, however; though, so far, his words have all been spelled correct.

I would hate to see you permanently injured, Henry, but I hope that when you try to tramp on the toes of a good boy simply because you are a seanyour and he is a fresh, as you frequently state, that he will arise and rip your little pleated jacket up the back and make your spinal colyum look like a corderoy bridge in the spring tra la. (This is from a Japan show I was to last week.)

Why should a seanyour in a colledge tromp onto the young chaps that come in there to learn? Have you forgot how I fatted up the old cow and beefed her so that you could go and monkey with youclid and algebray? Have you forgot how the other boys pulled you through a mill pond and made you tobogin down hill in a salt barrel with brads in it? Do you remember how your mother went down there to nuss you for two weeks and I stayed to home, and done my own work and the housework too and cooked my own vittles for the whole two weeks?

And now, Henry, you call yourself a seanyour, and therefore, because you are simply older in crime, you want to muss up Mr. Williams' features so that his mother will have to come over and nuss him. I am glad that your little pleated coat is ripped up the back, Henry, under the circumstances, and I am also glad that you are wearing the belt—over your off eye. If there's anything I can do to add to the hilarity of the occasion, please let me know and I will tend to it.

The lop-horned heifer is a parent once more, and I am trying in my poor, weak way to learn her wayward offspring how to drink out of a patent pail without pushing your old father over into the hay-mow. He is a cute little quadruped, with a wild desire to have fun at my expense. He loves to swaller a part of my coat-tail Sunday morning, when I am dressed up, and then return it to me in a moist condition. He seems to know that when I address the sabbath school the children will see the joke and enjoy it.

Your mother is about the same, trying in her meek way to adjust herself to a new set of teeth that are a size too large for her. She has one large bunion in the roof of her mouth already, but is still resolved to hold out faithful, and hopes these few lines will find you enjoying the same great blessing.

You will find inclosed a dark-blue money-order for four eighty-five. It is money that I had set aside to pay my taxes, but there is no novelty about paying taxes. I've done that before, so it don't thrill me as it used to.

Give my congratulations to Mr. Williams. He has got the elements of greatness to a wonderful degree. If I happened to be participating in that colledge of yours, I would gently but firmly decline to be tromped onto.

So good-bye for this time.

YOUR FATHER

From *Remarks By Bill Nye.*

A Mountain Snowstorm

September does not always indicate golden sunshine, and ripening corn, and old gold pumpkin pies on the half-shell. We look upon it as the month of glorious perfection in the handiwork of the seasons and the time when the ripened fruits are falling; when the red sun hides behind the bronze and misty evening, and says good night with reluctance to the beautiful harvests and the approaching twilight of the year.

It was on a red letter day of this kind, years ago, that Wheeler and myself started out under the charge of Judge Blair and Sheriff Boswell to visit the mines at Last Chance, and more especially the Keystone, a gold mine that the Judge had recently become president of. The soft air of second summer in the Rocky Mountains blew gently past our ears as we rode up the valley of the Little Laramie, to camp the first night at the head of the valley behind Sheep Mountain. The whole party was full of joy. Even Judge Blair, with the frosts of over sixty winters in his hair, broke forth into song. That's the only thing I ever had against Judge Blair. He would forget himself sometimes and burst forth into song.

The following day we crossed the divide and rode down the gulch into the camp on Douglas Creek, where the musical thunder of the stamp mills seemed to jar the ground, and the rapid stream below bore away on its turbid bosom the yellowish tinge of the golden quartz. It was a perfect day, and Wheeler and I blessed our stars, and, instead of breathing the air of sour paste and hot presses in the newspaper offices, away in the valley, we were sprawling in the glorious sunshine of the hills, playing draw poker with the miners in the evening, and forgetful of the daily newspaper where one man does the work and the other draws the salary. It was

172

heaven. It was such luxury that we wanted to swing our hats and yell like Arapahoes.

The next morning we were surprised to find that it had snowed all night and was snowing still. I never saw such flakes of snow in my life. They came sauntering through the air like pure, white Turkish towels falling from celestial clothes-lines. We did not return that day. We played a few games of chance, but they were brief. We finally made it five cent ante, and, as I was working then for an alleged newspaper man who paid me $50 per month to edit his paper nights and take care of his children daytimes, I couldn't keep abreast of the Judge, the Sheriff and the Superintendent of the Keystone.

The next day we had to go home. The snow lay ankle-deep everywhere and the air was chilly and raw. Wheeler and I tried to ride, but the mountain road was so rough that the horses could barely move through the snow, dragging the buggy after them. So we got out and walked on ahead to keep warm. We gained very fast on the team, for we were both long-legged and measured off the miles like a hired man going to dinner. I wore a pair of glove-fitting low shoes and lisle-thread socks. I can remember that yet. I would advise anyone going into the mines not to wear lisle-thread socks and low shoes. You are liable to stick your foot into a snow-bank or a mud hole and dip up too much water. I remember that after we had walked through the pine woods down the mountain road a few miles, I noticed that the bottoms of my pantaloons looked like those of a drowned tramp I saw many years ago in the morgue. We gave out after a while, waited for the team, but decided that it had gone the other road. All at once it flashed over us that we were alone in the woods and the storm, wet, nearly starved, ignorant of the road and utterly worn out!

It was tough!

I never felt so blue, so wet, so hungry, or so hopeless in my life. We moved on a little farther. All at once we came out of the timber. There was no snow whatever! At that moment the sun burst forth, we struck a deserted supply wagon, found a two-pound can of Boston baked beans, got an axe from the load, chopped open the can, and had just finished the tropical fruit of Massachusetts when our own team drove up, and joy and hope made their homes once more in our hearts.

We may learn from this a valuable lesson, but at this moment I do not know exactly what it is.

From *Remarks By Bill Nye.*

Nye and a Farmer by Eugene Zimmerman ("Zim")

Her Tired Hands

On board a western train the other day, I held in my bosom for over seventy-five miles, the elbow of a large man whose name I do not know. He was not a railroad hog or I would have resented it. He was built wide and he couldn't help it, so I forgave him.

He had a large, gentle, kindly eye, and when he desired to spit, he went to the car door, opened it and decorated the entire outside of the train forgetting that our speed would help to give scope to his remarks.

Naturally as he sat there by my side, holding on tightly to his ticket and evidently afraid that the conductor would forget to come and get it, I began to figure out in my mind what might be his business. He had pounded one thumb so that the nail was black where the blood had settled under it. This might happen to a shoemaker, a carpenter, a blacksmith or most any one else. So it didn't help me out much, though it looked to me as though it might have been done by trying to drive a fence-nail through a leather hinge with the back of an axe and nobody but a farmer would try to do that. Following up the clue, I discovered that he had milked on his boots and then I knew I was right. The man who milks before daylight, in a dark barn, when the thermometer is down to 28 degrees below and who hits his boot and misses the pail, by reason of the cold and the uncertain light and the prudishness of the cow, is a marked man. He cannot conceal the fact that he is a farmer unless he removes that badge. So I started out on that theory and remarked that this would pass for a pretty hard winter on stock.

The thought was not original with me, for I have heard it expressed by others either in this country or Europe. He said it would.

"My cattle has gone through a whole mowful o' hay since October and eleven ton o' brand. Hay don't seem to have the goodness to it thet it hed last year, and with their new *pro*-cess griss mills they jerk all the juice out o' brand, so's you might as well feed cows with excelsior and upholster your horses with hemlock bark as to buy brand."

"Well, why do you run so much to stock? Why don't you try diversified farming, and rotation of crops?"

"Well, probably you get that idee in the papers. A man that earns big wages writing Farm Hints for agricultural papers can make more money with a soft lead pencil and two or three season-cracked idees like that'n I can carrying of 'em out on the farm. We used to have a feller in the drugstore in our town that wrote such good pieces for the *Rural Vermonter* and made up such a good condition powder out of his own head, that two years ago we asked him to write a nessay for the annual meeting of the Buckwheat Trust, and use his own judgment about choice of subject. And what do you s'pose he had selected for a nessay that took the whole forenoon to read?"

"What subject, you mean?"

"Yes."

"Give it up!"

"Well, he'd wrote out that whole blamed intellectual wad on the subject of 'The Inhumanity of Dehorning Hydraulic Rams.' How's that?"

"That's pretty fair."

"Well, farmin' is like runnin' a paper in regards to some things. Every feller in the world will take and turn in and tell you how to do it, even if he don't know a blame thing about it. There ain't a man in the United States to-day that don't secretly think he could run airy one if his other business busted on him, whether he knows the difference between a new milch cow and a horse hay-rake or not. We had one of these embroidered night-shirt farmers come from town better'n three years ago. Been a toilet soap man and done well, and so he came out and bought a farm that had nothing to it but a fancy house and barn, a lot of medder in the front yard and a southern aspect. The farm was no good. You couldn't raise a disturbance on it. Well, what does he do? Goes and gits a passle of slim-tailed, yeller cows from New Jersey and aims to handle cream and diversified farming. Last year the cuss sent a load of cream over and tried to sell it at the new crematory while the funeral and hollercost was goin' on. I may be a sort of chump myself, but I read my paper and don't get left like that."

"What are the prospects for farmers in your State?"

"Well, they are pore. Never was so pore, in fact, sence I've been there. Folks wonder why boys leave the farm. My boys left so as to get protected, they said, and so they went into a clothing-store one of 'em, and one went into hardware and one is talking protection in the Legislature this winter. They said that farmin' was gittin' to be like fishin' and huntin', well enough for a man that has the means and leisure, but they couldn't make a livin' at it, they said. Another boy is in a drug store, and the man that hires him says he is a royal feller."

"Kind of a castor royal feller," I said, with a shriek of laughter.

He waited until I had laughed all I wanted to and then he said:

"I've always hollered for a high terriff in order to hyst the public debt, but now that we've got the national debt coopered I wish they'd take a little hack at mine. I've put in fifty years farmin'. I never drank licker in any form. I've worked from ten to eighteen hours a day, been economical in cloze and never went to a show more'n a dozen times in my life, raised a family and learned upward of two hundred calves to drink out of a tin pail without blowing all their vittles up my sleeve. My wife worked alongside o' me sewin' new seats on the boys' pants, skimmin' milk and even helpin' me load hay. For forty years we toiled along together and hardly got time to look into each others' faces or dared to stop and get acquainted with each other. Then her health failed. Ketched cold in the spring house, prob'ly skimmin' milk and washin' pans and scaldin' pails and spankin' butter. Anyhow, she took in a long breath one day while the doctor and me was watchin' her, and she says to me, 'Henry', says she, 'I've got a chance to rest,' and she put one tired, wore-out hand on top of the other tired, wore-out hand, and I knew she'd gone where they don't work all day and do chores all night.

"I took time to kiss her then. I'd been too busy for a good while previous to that, and then I called in the boys. After the funeral it was too much for them to stay around and eat the kind of cookin' we had to put up with, and nobody spoke up around the house as we used to. The boys quit whistlin' around the barn and talked kind of low by themselves about goin' to town and gettin' a job.

"They're all gone now and the snow is four feet deep on mother's grave up there in the old berryin' ground."

Then both of us looked out of the car window quite a long while without saying anything.

"I don't blame the boys for going into something else long's other things pays better; but I say—and I say what I know—that the man who holds the prosperity of this country in his hands, the man that actually makes money for other people to spend, the man that eats three good, simple, square meals a day and goes to bed at nine o'clock, so that future generations with good blood and cool brains can go from his farm to the Senate and Congress and the White House—he is the man that gets left at last to run his farm, with nobody to help him but a hired man and a high protective terriff. The farms in our State is mortgaged for over seven hundred million dollars. Ten of our Western States—I see by the papers—has got about three billion and a half mortgages on their farms, and that don't count the chattel mortgages filed with the town clerks on farm machinery, stock, waggins, and even crops, by gosh! that ain't two inches high under the snow. That's what the prospects is for farmers now. The Government is rich, but the men that made it, the men that fought perarie fires and perarie wolves and Injins and potato-bugs and blizzards, and has paid the war debt and pensions and everything else and hollered for the Union and the Republican party and free schools and high terriff and anything else that they was told to, is left high and dry this cold winter with a mortgage of seven billions and a half on the farms they have earned and saved a thousand times over."

"Yes; but look at the glory of sending from the farm the future President, the future Senator and the future member of Congress."

"That looks well on paper, but what does it really amount to? Soon as a farmer boy gits in a place like that he forgets the soil that produced him and holds his head as high as a hollyhock. He bellers for protection to everybody but the farmer, and while he sails round in a highty-tighty room with a fire in it night and day, his father on the farm has to kindle his own fire in the morning with elm slivvers, and he has to wear his son's lawn-tennis suit next to him or freeze to death, and he has to milk in an old gray shawl that has held that member of Congress when he was a baby, by gorry! and the old lady has to sojourn through the winter in the flannels that Silas wore at the riggatter before he went to Congress.

"So I say, and I think that Congress agrees with me, Damn a farmer, anyhow!"

He then went away.

From *Nye and Riley's Railway Guide*.

Where He First Met His Parents

Last week I visited my birthplace in the State of Maine. I waited thirty years for the public to visit it, and as there didn't seem to be much of a rush this spring, I thought I would go and visit it myself. I was telling a friend the other day that the public did not seem to manifest the interest in my birthplace that I thought it ought to, and he said I ought not to mind that. "Just wait," said he, " till the people of the United States have an opportunity to visit your tomb, and you will be surprised to see how they will run excursion trains up there to Moosehead lake, or wherever you plant yourself. It will be a perfect picnic. Your hold on the American people, William, is wonderful, but your death would seem to assure it, and kind of crystallize the affection now existing, but still in a nebulous and gummy state."

A man ought not to criticize his birthplace, I presume, and yet, if I were to do it all over again, I do not know whether I would select that particular spot or not. Sometimes I think I would not. And yet, what memories cluster about that old house! There was the place where I first met my parents. It was at that time that an acquaintance sprang up which has ripened in later years into mutual respect and esteem. It was there that what might be termed a casual meeting took place, that has, under the alchemy of resistless years, turned to golden links, forming a pleasant but powerful bond of union between my parents and myself. For that reason, I hope that I may be spared to my parents for many years to come.

Many memories now cluster about that old home, as I have said. There is, also, other bric-a-brac which has accumulated since I was born there. I took a small stone from the front yard as a kind of memento of the occasion and the place. I do not think it

Nye Contemplating His Birthplace by Eugene Zimmerman ("Zim")

has been detected yet. There was another stone in the yard, so it may be weeks before any one finds out that I took one of them.

How humble the home, and yet what a lesson it should teach the boys of America! Here, amid the barren and inhospitable waste of rocks and cold, the last place in the world that a great man would naturally select to be born in, began the life of one who, by his own unaided effort, in after years rose to the proud height of postmaster at Laramie City, Wy. T., and with an estimate of the future that seemed almost prophetic, resigned before he could be characterized as an offensive partisan.

Here on the banks of the raging Piscataquis, where winter lingers in the lap of spring till it occasions a good deal of talk, there began a career which has been the wonder and admiration of every vigilance committee west of the turbulent Missouri.

There on that spot, with no inheritance but a predisposition to baldness and a bitter hatred of rum; with no personal property but a misfit suspender and a stone-bruise, began a life history which has never ceased to be a warning to people who have sold goods on credit.

It should teach the youth of our great, broad land what glorious possibilities may lie concealed in the rough and tough bosom of the reluctant present. It shows how steady perseverance and a good appetite will always win in the end. It teaches us that wealth is not indispensable, and that if we live as we should, draw out of politics at the proper time, and die a few days before the public absolutely demand it, the matter of our birthplace will not be considered.

Still, my birthplace is all right as a birthplace. It was a good, quiet place in which to be born. All the old neighbors said that Shirley was a very quiet place up to the time I was born there, and when I took my parents by the hand and gently led them away in the spring of '53, saying, "Parents, this is no place for us," it again became quiet.

It is the only birthplace I have, however, and I hope that all the readers of this sketch will feel perfectly free to go there any time and visit it and carry their dinner as I did. Extravagant cordiality and overflowing hospitality have always kept my birthplace back.

From *Nye and Riley's Railway Guide.*

No More Frontier

The system of building railroads into the wilderness, and then allowing the wilderness to develop afterward, has knocked the essential joy out of the life of the pioneer. At one time the hardy hewer of wood and drawer of water gave his lifetime willingly that his son might ride in the "varnished cars." Now the Pullman palace car takes the New Yorker to the threshold of the sea, or to the boundary line between the United States and the British possessions.

It has driven out the long handled frying pan and the flapjack of twenty years ago, and introduced the condensed milk and canned fruit of commerce. Along the highways, where once the hopeful hundreds marched with long handled shovel and pick and pan, cooking by the way thin salt pork and flapjacks and slumgullion, now the road is lined with empty beer bottles and peach cans that have outlived their usefulness. No landscape can be picturesque with an empty peach can in the foreground any more than a lion would look grand in a red monogram horse blanket and false teeth.

The modern camp is not the camp of the wilderness. It wears the half-civilized and shabby genteel garments of a sawed-off town. You know that if you ride a day you will be where you can get the daily papers and read them under the electric light. That robs the old canyons of their solemn isolation and peoples each gulch with the odor of codfish balls and civilization. Civilization is not to blame for all this, and yet it seems sad.

Civilization could not have done all this alone. It had to call to its aid the infernal fruit can that now desolates the most obscure trail in the heart of the mountains. You walk over chaos where the "hydraulic" has plowed up the valley like a convulsion, or you

182

tread the yielding path across the deserted dump, and on all sides the rusty, neglected and humiliated empty tin can stares at you with its monotonous, dude-like stare.

An old timer said to me once: "I've about decided, Bill, that the West is a matter of history. When we cooked our grub over a sage brush fire we could get fat and fight Indians, but now we fill our digesters with the cold pizen and pewter of the canned peach; we go to a big tavern and stick a towel under our chins and eat pie with a fork and heat up our carkisses with anti-christ coal, and what do we amount to? Nuthin! I used to chase Injuns all day and eat raw salt pork at night, bekuz I dassent build a fire, and still I felt better than I do now with a wad of tin-can solder in my stummick and a homesick feeling in my weather-beaten breast.

"No, we don't have the fun we used to. We have more swarrees and sciatica and one bloomin' thing and another of that kind, but we don't get one snort of pure air and appetite in a year. They're bringin' in their blamed telephones now and malaria and aigue and old sledge, and fun might as well skip out. There ain't no frontier any more. All we've got left is the old-fashioned trantler joos and rhumatiz of '49."

> Behind the red squaw's cayuse plug,
>   The hand-car roars and raves,
> And pie-plant pies are now produced
>   Above the Indian graves.
> I hear the oaths of pioneers,
>   The caucus yet to be,
> The first low hum where soon will come
>   the fuzzy bumble bee.

From *Remarks By Bill Nye*.